WHY EVERY THERAPIST MUST WRITE A BOOK

"How to Use a Book as a Strategy"

RAAM ANAND

STARDOM BOOKS

www.StardomBooks.com

STARDOM BOOKS
112 Bordeaux Ct.
Coppell, TX 75019, USA

Copyright © 2025 by RAAM ANAND

All rights reserved. No part of this book may be reproduced or used in any manner without written permission of the copyright owner except for the use of quotations in a book review.

FIRST EDITION NOVEMBER 2025

STARDOM BOOKS, LLC.
112 Bordeaux Ct. Coppell, TX 75019, USA

www.stardombooks.com

Stardom Books, United States
Stardom Alliance, India

The author and publishers have made all reasonable efforts to contact copyright holders for permission and apologize for any omissions or errors in the form of credits given. Corrections may be made to future editions.

WHY EVERY THERAPIST MUST WRITE A BOOK
"How to Use a Book as a Strategy"

RAAM ANAND

p. 151
cm. 13.5 X 21.5

Category: LAN027000 LANGUAGE ARTS & DISCIPLINES/
Publishers & Publishing Industry
BUS043000 Business / Economics : Marketing - General

ISBN: 978-1-957456-82-9

Dedication

To the therapists who hold space for healing, listen with compassion, and guide others toward light in their darkest moments. This book is dedicated to your courage, empathy, and unwavering commitment to the emotional well-being of others. This is a small token of appreciation for the profound impact you make — one session, one story, one soul at a time. May this work inspire you to charter new territories in your practice, leadership, and in the narratives, you choose to share.

Acknowledgements

Gratitude is the heart's memory, and this book pulses with appreciation for many. To my family, for their patience and belief in the power of storytelling, I am forever grateful—my sincerest thanks to the therapists whose experiences and insights have been the bedrock of my journey.

I extend my profound appreciation to the team at Stardom Books, who warrant a special mention for their strategic support and steadfast accountability that steered this project to its completion. Finally, to you, the reader, embarking on this written voyage, may you find in these pages the spark to ignite your author ambitions.

Contents

Introduction	1
1. Elevating Your Professional Status	17
2. Expanding Your Professional Network	31
3. Enhancing Client Relationships	49
4. Boosting Your Therapy Practice's Reputation	65
5. Personal and Professional Fulfilment	81
6. Strategic Community Growth	95
7. How & Where to Get Professional Help	111
Putting It All Together	129
About the Author	141

Introduction

"Writing is medicine. It is an appropriate antidote to injury. It is an appropriate companion for any difficult change."

— **Julia Cameron**

You may have already helped others speak their truth and confront the ones they've been holding inside. But what about *your* truth?

At the heart of a therapist's work lies a central objective; a foundation that supports their professional practice. While many mental health professionals begin their careers in pursuit of financial stability, their deeper motivation is always the same: to serve and to help. In every therapeutic encounter, you witness transformation, sometimes subtle, sometimes life-changing. But what if your insights could reach audiences beyond your private practice?

Writing a book is not simply a task; it is a transformative journey. It allows you to extend your reach, amplify your message, and create a legacy. A book is both a personal accomplishment and a professional tool—one that builds lasting influence and recognition. This journey is not just about putting words on a page; it is about realizing your potential and the impact you can have.

In recent years, self-help books, memoirs, and psychology titles have risen to extraordinary popularity.

Readers are searching for validation for their feelings, understanding, and practical tools. While blogs, podcasts, and social media thrive, many still turn to books for the depth, permanence, and authority they provide. Consider how leaders in the field like Brené Brown, Esther Perel, and Gabor Maté have extended their influence far beyond their sessions through writing.

As a therapist, you already possess qualities that make you uniquely equipped to write a meaningful book: deep listening, clear articulation, emotional intelligence, and lived insight. You don't need to be a literary genius. You only need the willingness to share what you know in your authentic voice. The writing process is accessible to you, and this book is here to guide you through it.

From discovering your core message to overcoming imposter syndrome and navigating the publishing process, you'll learn how to transform your professional expertise into a published book; one that reflects your values and amplifies your visibility.

You don't need anyone's permission to begin. What you need is clarity, strategy, and courage. So, let's start.

Becoming a therapist is more than a career choice; it is a calling. You entered this field to help, to heal, and to hold space for growth. Whether you work in private practice, a clinic, a hospital, or a community setting, the lives you touch undergo meaningful change. However, even change has limits. Your time, energy, and influence are limited.

But what if your wisdom, stories, and voice could reach not just one person at a time, but hundreds, thousands, or even millions? What if your words could outlast your sessions—and even your lifetime?

That is the power of a book.

Still, the questions linger: *Where do you begin? Is there room for your story?* If you've spent years immersed in clinical practice, the idea of writing may feel distant, even daunting. The pressure of deadlines and the fear of appearing self-indulgent can hold you back.

However, therapists' voices are more essential than ever in today's conversations about mental health.

In the wake of the global pandemic, the demand for trustworthy, accessible guidance has surged. Readers are turning to books in record numbers; not just for knowledge, but for connection. They want to feel seen, understood, and guided by professionals who offer both expertise and empathy.

Purpose of This Book

Your book could help bridge the gap between what is clinically known and what the public believes, thereby lessening stigma and empowering. For a therapist, writing a book is more than a personal challenge. It is a responsibility, an opportunity to demystify therapy, share clinical insights with the public, and reach people you may never meet. A book provides access to those who cannot afford therapy, do not know how to ask for help, or live in communities where stigma keeps them silent. It is about creating ripples that will grow into waves of change.

Each chapter has the potential to educate, normalize, empower, and heal. You do not need to be a celebrity or strive for perfection; you only need the willingness to share your wisdom. Therapists are natural storytellers who witness transformation every day. Now is the time to create, reflect, and distill your stories, strategies, and lessons into a format that reaches a wider audience and extends across time, helping more people in meaningful ways.

You already have the talent, passion, and perspective to make an impact. Writing a book allows you to amplify that impact, reaching readers far beyond your practice. As an author, you have the opportunity to create an experience that educates, inspires, and leaves a lasting impression long after the final page is turned.

This book, *Why Every Therapist Must Write a Book: How to Use a Book as a Strategy,* is designed to guide you through the writing process from inception to publication. You will learn how to shape your message, identify your audience, and organize your ideas into a book that resonates with readers. You do not need to be a professional writer or have flawless grammar; what matters most is clarity, purpose, and the desire to share your knowledge. This book is your navigational guide to making authorship possible. Along the way, you will also discover how to manage common challenges and apply practical strategies to overcome them. By the end, you will not only understand the writing and publishing process, but also the strategic benefits of having your work in print.

Why Writing a Book is Beneficial for Therapists

Therapists, especially those in private practice or building their public presence, often seek greater visibility, credibility, and deeper connections with the right clients. Writing a book is a powerful way to achieve all of these goals. More importantly, it serves as a tool for professional development, advocacy, and reaching an audience far beyond the field of therapy. It is visionary thinking for the future.

In today's world of endless content, trust and visibility matter more than ever. Many potential clients begin their search for support online before they ever reach out.

A book allows you to showcase your therapeutic philosophy, demonstrate your style, and build authentic connections with potential clients across digital platforms.

Here are a few reasons why writing a book can be especially beneficial for therapists:

- **Establishing Credibility and Authority:** A book positions you as a trusted expert in your niche, whether it is trauma therapy, couples counseling, adolescent mental health, or another specialty. It distinguishes you from other practitioners and affirms your expertise and leadership. Published work increases trust and enhances the likelihood of recommendations from colleagues, clients, and even media outlets.

- **Expanding Professional Networks**: Books open doors to new opportunities, including speaking engagements, workshops, podcasts, and collaborations. As an author, you are more likely to be invited to conferences and professional gatherings. Your book becomes a resource that builds connections with therapists, educators, organizations, and influential voices in mental health.

- **Enhancing Marketing and Branding**: For many therapist-authors, a book becomes a cornerstone of their professional identity. It strengthens your personal brand, helps you communicate your message clearly, and extends your influence in a field where trust is everything.

- **Personal and Professional Satisfaction**: Writing a book can be a milestone that deepens both reflection and growth. It allows you to revisit your values, consolidate your insights, and appreciate your professional journey. Many therapists find the writing process itself healing and transformative. Sharing your story creates a broader impact and often brings profound personal fulfillment.

- **Growth of Strategic Practices**: A book can directly contribute to expanding your practice. Beyond sales, it can generate new opportunities such as consulting, speaking engagements, workshops, and online courses. These avenues not only attract clients but also create sustainable revenue streams.

In a world where people crave clarity, comfort, and guidance, your voice matters. Your book can offer readers insights, perspective, and hope during their most vulnerable moments. It is not about having all the answers. It is about sharing what you know in a way that makes people feel heard, understood, and empowered.

How This Book Will Help You

This book is designed to be your supportive and motivational ally on the path to becoming a published therapist-author. Each chapter focuses on a specific aspect of the writing journey, tailored to the unique needs, challenges, and aspirations of therapists. This palette of support will help you articulate your message, develop your author persona, and expand your influence far beyond the therapy room, regardless whether you work in private practice, a clinic, or a larger organization.

Here's a quick preview of what to expect:

Chapter 1: Elevating Your Professional Status: Discover how publishing a book can establish you as an authority in your field. You will explore how authorship builds credibility with clients, peers, institutions, and the media, and how it helps you stand out in a trust-driven profession like therapy.

Chapter 2: Expanding Your Professional Network: Learn how a book can unlock professional relationships that once seemed out of reach. Authorship becomes a catalyst for collaboration, opening doors to speaking engagements, joint ventures, media features, and peer recommendations.

Chapter 3: Enhancing Client Relationships: Explore how your book can strengthen therapeutic connections. You'll see how it answers common questions, fosters trust even before the first session, and serves as a lasting resource that supports retention and deeper engagement.

Chapter 4: Boosting Your Practice's Reputation: Understand how a book can serve as the cornerstone of your brand. You'll learn strategies to attract attention, increase visibility, and position yourself as a respected authority in your area of expertise.

Chapter 5: Personal and Professional Fulfillment: Reflect on the deeper rewards of authorship. This chapter highlights how writing a book nurtures self-expression, confidence, and growth, while offering a process that can be healing, empowering, and transformative.

Chapter 6: Strategic Community Growth: See how your book can serve as a long-term strategic asset. From workshops and content marketing to lead generation and consulting opportunities, you'll uncover ways to use your book to expand your platform and practice sustainably.

Chapter 7: How & Where to Get Professional Help: Gain insight into publishing services and resources designed to support you throughout your authorship journey, from manuscript to market.

Within these pages, you'll find the perspectives of therapists who have walked this path before, supported by research, expert insights, and step-by-step guidance. Whether you are just beginning to imagine your book or are already deep into your manuscript, this book will meet you where you are and help you move forward with clarity, confidence, and purpose

Why Your Expertise Belongs in Print

Consider the path of Dr. Susan David, author of *Emotional Agility* and psychologist at Harvard Medical School. Before publishing her book, Dr. David's research on psychological flexibility, emotional resilience, and emotional wellness was already well-regarded within academic and clinical circles. However, it was the publication of *Emotional Agility* that brought her ideas to a national stage. 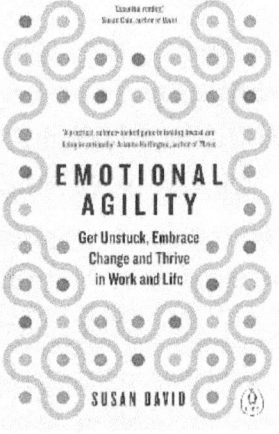 The book became a bestseller, was listed among the best business books by the *Harvard Business Review*, and opened doors to speaking engagements, TED Talks, and podcasts across corporate and mental health spaces. By translating complex psychological concepts into relatable, practical tools, Dr. David bridged the gap between academia and everyday life, ultimately establishing herself as a leading voice in emotional wellness.

In a similar way, clinical psychologist and professor Dr. Jordan Peterson rose to international prominence following the release of his book *12 Rules for Life: An Antidote to Chaos*. While he already had a strong academic following, the book's success, and the extensive publicity surrounding it, propelled his reach onto the global stage. Selling more than ten million copies, it sparked worldwide conversations and led to sold-out lecture tours, media appearances, and influential discussions. Blending philosophy, mythology, and therapeutic principles, Peterson's work positioned him as a thought leader at the intersection of culture, psychology, and personal development.

These examples demonstrate how writing a book can profoundly shape the trajectory of your career. Sharing your therapeutic insights, clinical experiences, and skills not only educates and empowers readers but also elevates your professional profile and expands your reach. Authorship creates opportunities for meaningful conversations that influence both practice and public perception.

For therapists, writing a book is not simply about adding the title of "author" to your name. It is about sharing your expertise, understanding the importance of having your voice heard, and creating a legacy that extends far beyond you. Readers across time zones, countries, and cultures can engage with your ideas, even if they have never stepped into a therapy session with you.

That is the true power of authorship, and it is entirely within your reach.

Understanding the Strategic Advantages of Authorship

Controlling your professional narrative is one of the key strategic advantages of writing a book. A book allows you to shape how you are perceived, whether as a therapist, a thought leader, or a trusted voice—in today's fast-paced and competitive mental health marketplace, where online presence and social proof carry enormous weight. Through authorship, you can communicate your clinical reflections and theoretical perspectives while authentically representing your experience and practice. Unlike a certificate, a short presentation, or a testimonial, a book uniquely influences how your audience perceives your professional accountability and credibility.

A book is also a long-term marketing and branding vehicle. A blog post or social media update may have impact for a moment, but a book can be talked about, quoted, shared, promoted, and cited for decades. Its longevity allows you to build a personal brand that grows in value over time rather than fading away.

Dr. Harriet Lerner, a clinical psychologist and author of the groundbreaking book *The Dance of Anger*, is a clear example of this. Before publication, Lerner was already respected within academic and therapeutic communities. Yet it was her book that made her a household name. Written in a style that was both brilliant and conversational, *The Dance of Anger* helped countless women understand their anger and, more importantly, respond to it in healthier and more empowering ways. Millions of readers worldwide purchased the book, which continues to be translated into multiple languages and remains a bestseller decades later. The book not only gave Lerner public recognition but also expanded the reach of her therapeutic concepts. She went on to become a sought-after speaker, her ideas were integrated into therapy practices around the globe, and her books became essential reading for both clients and professionals. Lerner emerged as a therapist, thought leader, teacher, and cultural authority in the areas of emotional health and gender.

Writing a book can have the same effect for today's therapists. It broadens your scope, sharpens your message, and positions you as an expert. In a profession where trust is vital and knowledge is your currency, a well-written book is the most powerful calling card you can create.

Case Study: Dr. Kelly McGonigal

As a psychologist and a Professor at Stanford University, Dr. Kelly McGonigal has an extensive and impactful history as a researcher and practitioner in the areas of willpower, stress, and movement psychology. Although Dr. McGonigal was already a part of the conversation in the academy and clinical practice, her books, especially *The Willpower Instinct* (2011) and *The Upside of Stress* (2015), raised her to international prominence and changed the trajectory of her career. Her first trade book, The Willpower Instinct, combines ideas from neuroscience, psychology, and examples from society to offer an entertaining and scientifically robust account of self-control (an issue with which both therapists and clients struggle). The book quickly became a hit with readers from all walks of life, not only because of its delightful content, but because of Dr. McGonigal's unique voice—concise, mindful, and human.

She has a talent for summarizing complex psychological theories into straightforward behavioral recommendations that readers can apply immediately—a trait many therapists share, but seldom express as clearly in written form.

After launching her book, Dr. McGonigal began to be invited to speak at major conferences, appear in media outlets, and contribute to platforms such as TED, The New York Times, and The Wall Street Journal. As of late 2023, her TED Talk on stress from her second book, The Upside of Stress, had surpassed 25 million views, and she had become a recognized thought leader in the field of stress management. The book challenged the conventional health psychology idea that stress is purely bad for us. Dr. McGonigal proposed that reframing stress has the potential to transform the outcomes of stress from debilitating to using stress as a meaningful impetus for growth, interdependence, and resilience. Her message was timely, audacious, and controversial, but all the research was solid, and she delivered it in an authentic, empathetic, and nuanced way, making the book relatable. Therapists began using her frameworks in their sessions, coaches adopted her ideas in their seminars, and organizations began requesting training from her for their staff.

The evolution of Dr. Kelly McGonigal as an author reveals how one can change in ways they never imagined. Writing books allowed her to publicly demonstrate her expertise and establish a connection between her specialized knowledge — whether personal, professional, or intellectual — and the broader world.

Dr. McGonigal became a thought leader; she utilized her expertise as a clinician and her unique skill at communication to help others when they needed it.

If you are a therapist wondering if writing a book might be worth the investment of time and energy, Dr. McGonigal has a story that demonstrates why it can be a career-changing process. Her pathway shows that if you merge your ideas with purpose and clarity, you can produce a book that leads you to avenues you never would have even dreamt of. It allows you to project your voice, widen your influence, and embody your public persona.

Writing a book can feel intimidating, yet it is one of the most powerful and enduring ways to expand your therapeutic work beyond the counseling room. At its core, all it requires is the desire to share your knowledge with people who need it most. Your words can become the lifeline a reader is searching for, the comfort that helps them feel seen, supported, and guided as they begin their healing journey, even if you never meet them in person.

Your lived experiences, combined with your clinical expertise and human insight, are invaluable assets. When transformed into a book, they become a tool for advocacy, education, and empowerment. Through writing, you can raise awareness about mental health, provide readers with practical strategies, and give a voice to those who feel isolated or unheard. The therapeutic work of helping others understand their narrative becomes accessible to the entire world through writing.

Writing a book is more than professional recognition. It is both an act of service and an act of courage, one that makes a lasting contribution to the lives of others.

It preserves your voice, strengthens the values that led you into this work, and extends your influence far beyond the therapy room.

You do not need to wait for perfection, permission, or the "right" moment. Your story, your wisdom, and your voice are already enough. Through authorship, you step into the dual role of healer and messenger; someone whose impact can reach beyond a single session, a single client, or even a single lifetime.

Key Takeaways

- A book lets you reach past the therapy space by providing help to people who would never have access to traditional methods of support.

- A published book builds your authority and trust, while standing out from others in a competitive market requires differentiation and credibility.

- Writing a book enhances your branding and opens up professional opportunities, as well as attracting pursuits that align with your goals.

- Remember, you don't need to be perfect; willingness to share your knowledge is enough, and you can begin writing.

This guide serves as both a reference and a companion, showing you the lasting impact that purposeful words and heartfelt messages can have beyond your workplace. Your words carry the power to reach far past the walls of your office when shaped with intention and care. You already hold all the elements needed to become an agent of change.

The next step is to transform your insights into an enduring message; one that readers can return to again and again as they continue to learn and grow. The sections ahead will walk you through the process of building that message.

Your journey begins now.

Chapter 1

Elevating Your Professional Status

"Reading maketh a full man; conference a ready man; and writing an exact man."

— **Francis Bacon**

It's exactly 11:47 p.m., and her third cup of herbal tea has gone cold. She has tried journaling, deep breathing, even scrolling through social media, but nothing lifts the weight from her chest. It isn't panic exactly, more like a slow, steady pressure. A quiet sense that her life has slipped off the rails and she no longer know how to steer it back.

She opens her laptop, hesitates at the search bar, then types: *"therapist near me for anxiety."* What she's really searching for isn't a therapist. It's something less clinical, something harder to name: safety, understanding, trust.

The results appear. Profile after profile. Degrees. Certifications. Years of experience. All impressive, yet all strangely impersonal. None of it cuts through the fog—until something catches her eye.

One therapist has written a book.

It isn't the title or even the cover that draws her in. It's the presence behind it. The thoughtfulness. She reads a few paragraphs from the sample and recognizes something rare: a voice that feels calm, real, and grounded.

Not just someone who treats anxiety, but someone who understands it. In that moment, she feels connection. Relief. A flicker of safety.

And in that moment, she stops searching. She's found someone she can trust enough to reach out to.

Every therapist would like to be that person. Clients begin building trust long before their first session. Sometimes in a phone call, often through a website, and increasingly through the content they find online. Yet many good therapists never reach that point, not because they lack skill, but because their *voice* is missing. A book changes that. It becomes the single most powerful tool for building trust with clients and establishing authority before they ever meet you.

It isn't always about being the best; it's about perceived as the best. That's the essence of authority in today's world. Your online presence is your first impression, and potential clients are already checking you out, reading your content, comparing your reviews, and weighing you against the next tab.

The real question is this: how do you move from being one of many to becoming the one they choose?

In this chapter, we will explore how to build presence and power—not through tools or devices, but through something far more sustainable: authorship. Writing a book in your field is never just about the book itself. It becomes living evidence of your knowledge and a fast track to trust. It gives people a reason to believe in you before you ever meet them.

Authorship is a catalyst that can transform your professional experience, elevate your reputation, and help you grow into possibilities greater than you may have imagined. Most importantly, it empowers you to speak your voice to the world.

Establishing Authority

Dr. Bessel van der Kolk is a psychiatrist, therapist, and researcher widely known for his pioneering work on post-traumatic stress disorder (PTSD) and the effects of trauma on the brain and body. Often called the father of trauma therapy, he is trusted by both colleagues and clients alike. His journey illustrates the power of sharing clinical knowledge with the world through  research, public talks, and, most notably, writing. His book *The Body Keeps the Score: Brain, Mind, and Body in the Healing of Trauma* not only educated readers but also established him as one of the most respected voices in the field of mental health.

The impact is undeniable. To be known, respected, and visible to both peers and the public is a powerful achievement. Media outlets, institutions, and audiences now look to him as a guide. This is what defines a thought leader: someone whose expertise and insights help shape the way others think and act. True thought leaders are more than experts; they are creative, authentic voices whose honesty builds trust and credibility.

So, how did Dr. van der Kolk move from being a practicing psychiatrist to becoming a global thought leader?

He changed the way people understood trauma. Before his work gained prominence, PTSD was often treated primarily with medication and framed as a cognitive issue. After nearly three decades of research and clinical practice, he highlighted how trauma disrupts brain development and becomes embedded in the body. Concerned about the limitations of medication, he began exploring safer and more integrative treatments.

In *The Body Keeps the Score*, he introduced body-based healing approaches such as EMDR, yoga, neurofeedback, and somatic experiencing.

The result was groundbreaking. The book became an international bestseller, staying on the *New York Times* and Amazon bestseller lists for more than 300 weeks and being translated into over forty languages. It resonated deeply with both professionals and general readers. Patient stories made the science accessible and relatable, while his call for holistic, whole-person recovery shifted the global conversation on trauma care.

Dr. van der Kolk's journey shows the transformative potential of authorship. By sharing his insights with the world, he not only influenced his profession but also changed countless lives.

> **Research Article v/s Book**
>
> There are many reasons to write a book instead of an article. Both can help you build authority and show your knowledge, skills, and experience. That said, the type of authority is different. When you publish an article, you become seen as an expert within your professional community and as an academic or scientific voice. A book puts you in the space of a thought leader who builds trust with both the public and other professionals.
>
> Research papers are typically read by academics, researchers, or practicing clinicians in your field, behind a paywall or otherwise limited. A book can be read by a much broader audience, including clients, colleagues, the media, and the general public. Books are much easier to access through libraries, bookstores, or online. They also provide more opportunities for exposure and income generation.

> Research articles will net you things like academic promotions, journal invites, or research collaborations. A book can lead to media interviews, speaking engagements, or even podcast invitations. A book is also a credible form of social proof. A book will also enhance your practice and ultimately, your brand. For example, Dr. Bessel has written many empirical research articles, but it is the book he published that made him a thought leader. A book represents much more than a publication. A book is another way to prove that you are credible and that you have earned a spot in your field.

Dr. George S. Everly Jr. is a clinical psychologist, academic, and pioneer in the field of disaster mental health. He has years of experience working with crisis teams, first responders, and military personnel around the world. As a co-founder of the International Critical Incident Stress Foundation (ICISF), Dr. Everly helped create psychological first aid techniques that are now part of emergency response systems in many countries. His book *The Johns Hopkins Guide to Psychological First Aid*, co-authored with Dr. Jeffrey Lating, is used as a manual to teach crisis skills and trauma-aware communication to police, fire, and EMS teams. Today, it is far more than an academic resource—it is a trusted guide applied in real-world emergencies.

Beyond professional training, Dr. Everly's other works, such as *Stronger: Develop the Resilience You Need to Succeed*, have reached corporate leaders as well as the general public.

These books have led to speaking invitations from FEMA, the FBI, and organizations in more than 25 countries. His influence comes not only from years of clinical expertise but also from his ability to distill that knowledge into clear, practical resources that first responders and professionals can put to use immediately.

In any field, publishing a book is a powerful marker of credibility. It demonstrates not only what you know but also your ability to follow through on a significant project. Writing a book requires time, focus, and discipline. Unlike posting a blog or hosting a webinar, it demands structure, clarity of thought, and a message that resonates. A book shows that you can take complex ideas and make them understandable. That gives clients something beyond your credentials. It gives them clarity and trust.

Publishing a book is ultimately a gift to three groups: the public, your profession, and yourself. To the public, it shares your insights and makes mental health concepts easier to understand, while helping future clients recognize whom they want to work with. The stories within can also reassure readers that they are not alone. To professionals, a research-backed book can contribute new tools and approaches to the field. And for you, the author, it builds authority, visibility, and long-term value.

Even though the pandemic made conversations about mental health more open, stigma still lingers. Every honest discussion helps break that barrier. A book amplifies your voice, grows your career, and positions you as a trusted authority. It increases visibility, strengthens reputation, and expands your reach. Esther Perel is a great example of this. Her one book was enough to elevate her career to an entirely new level.

The Journey of Esther Perel

Just as Dr. Everly used his writing to bring trauma-informed care into emergency protocols, Esther Perel used her voice to start a global conversation about desire in long-term relationships. Esther Perel is the daughter of Polish-Jewish parents who survived the Holocaust. Growing up with stories of trauma, survival, and the human mind sparked her early interest in psychology. She trained as a psychotherapist and began her practice in New York, focusing on relationships. For years, she had a steady practice and was known within her circles. But she noticed that no one was talking about the decline of desire in long-term relationships. Most therapists focused on attachment and communication, but Esther felt that was only part of the story. She began exploring how to keep desire alive over time, which was a more profound and more challenging idea.

In 2006, Esther published her first book, *Mating in Captivity: Unlocking Erotic Intelligence*. The book was not only innovative and thought-provoking but also stirred up a lot of discussion. It pushed back against therapy models that focused only on interpreting behaviors. Instead, it encouraged couples to bring mystery, imagination, and space into their relationships. The book was translated into more than 25 languages and sold hundreds of thousands of copies. With its personal tone, stories, and real case examples, it stood out among many other titles on the topic.

> After publishing her book, Esther went from being a therapist to becoming a global expert on relationships. Her credibility grew, leading to speaking invitations at international events. Her 2013 TED talk, *The Secret to Desire in a Long-Term Relationship*, gained over 8 million views, and her second TED talk on the same topic reached more than 15 million. Esther didn't bring attention to the topic. She started a real global conversation. She went on to launch a podcast, give interviews, and write articles. Today, she is a respected voice and leader in her field. She leads workshops around the world, trains other therapists, and has helped millions of couples. Her credibility lifted her career and brought fresh thinking to her field. And it all started with one bold move. She wrote a book.

Benefits of Authority

The examples of Esther Perel and Dr. Bessel van der Kolk show how one book can shape not only a career but also an entire field. Being recognized as an authority brings real, lasting benefits. A book is not just evidence of what you know—it is also a demonstration of trust, dedication, and long-term value. It makes your credibility visible and enduring. Once published, a book often prompts others to seek your advice, request consultations, and create new opportunities for growth.

From Esther's story, we see that publishing her first book opened doors to invitations from organizations worldwide eager to hear her insights. While every journey is unique, becoming a published author frequently leads to media coverage, speaking engagements, and other opportunities for professional development. Think of the therapists who lead workshops or appear in feature articles—most of them are authors.

Their books convey expertise in ways that extend their influence far beyond the therapy room. Writing a book may not guarantee success, but it significantly increases the likelihood that your voice will be heard by a broader audience.

As a therapist, your work already helps people heal and grow, often one person at a time. Yet you may have felt that many more could benefit from your knowledge. Writing a book is one of the best ways to reach them.

It allows you to connect with larger groups and makes it far more likely that journalists or media outlets will seek your perspective for interviews and articles. With that exposure, your message can touch far more lives than individual sessions alone ever could.

Publishing also helps you attract the right clients. Not every therapist is the right fit for every individual, and that is natural. But when someone reads your book and recognizes their own struggles in your words, they are more likely to reach out. This creates a meaningful alignment: you connect with clients whose needs match your strengths, and they find the therapist best suited to help them. Both sides benefit.

The benefits go beyond client work. Writing a book can also open doors in academic and professional settings, as shown by Dr. Irvin Yalom. His book *Theory and Practice of Group Psychotherapy* became a widely used textbook, and he was invited to contribute more to academic writing.

The same could happen to you. Publishing a book helps you build authority and can lead to many new opportunities. It is something worth considering.

Building Credibility

Credibility comes from being believable, trustworthy, and skilled. Most doctors build their credibility through years of work and by building a strong client history.

But this can be a long process and may not always lead to results. Writing a book can speed that up. Being published shows that you are an expert in your field and that others can trust your knowledge. It gives clients more confidence in your work.

Imagine receiving two papers—one written by a professor and another by a student—each presenting a different view on the same topic. Whose perspective would you trust more? Most people would choose the professor, simply because they are seen as the expert.

Now, imagine that both papers were written by professors. The decision becomes harder. But if one of those professors has also published a book on the subject, that author is far more likely to earn your trust, even if both hold the same degree. The same principle applies to therapists. Having a book makes you stand out and signals to others that you are a trusted authority.

A powerful example of how personal storytelling can build professional credibility is Lori Gottlieb's journey. In an interview, the psychotherapist and New York Times bestselling author explained how her book *Maybe You Should Talk to Someone* transformed her career.

By openly sharing her experiences as both a therapist and a patient, she reached a far wider audience and built deep trust with readers. Following the book's release, she attracted more clients and received numerous invitations to appear on media platforms.

Building Credibility

While Lori built trust through honesty and personal stories, Gabor Maté earned respect through clinical insight and innovative approaches. Already recognized for his groundbreaking work in addiction and trauma, his influence expanded dramatically after publishing *In the Realm of Hungry Ghosts* in 2008. The book not only strengthened his credibility but also became widely used by therapists, psychologists, and doctors, many of whom recommend it to their clients even today.

So why does a book have this kind of power? One reason lies in the way people form trust. Robert Cialdini explores this idea in his classic work on social proof, *Influence: The Psychology of Persuasion*. He explains that when people feel uncertain, they often look to the choices of others to guide their own. We are more inclined to trust people or resources that others already trust.

Now consider this from the perspective of a client; let's call her Nancy. Nancy is searching for a therapist, but she doesn't know where to start. She feels vulnerable and wants to be sure she finds someone she can trust. She checks reviews, reads articles, and asks for recommendations. Then she discovers a book written by you. The book has strong reviews and outlines specific outcomes. Nancy might think, *"If so many people trust this therapist, I can trust them too."* That sense of social proof gives her the confidence and certainty to reach out.

If you've ever wondered whether you have something worth writing about, consider this: your clients already see you as someone who listens, helps, and brings healing. That alone means you have something valuable to share. The stories, lessons, and breakthroughs you witness in the therapy room are more than session notes—they hold insight. And when shaped into a book, that insight can reach far beyond your practice and touch lives you may never meet in person.

You don't need to be famous. You don't need to have all the answers. What you need is the courage to say, *"What I know could help someone else."* Because it can.

Writing a book isn't about self-promotion, it's about service. It's about offering hope to someone struggling at 11:47 p.m., unsure where to turn. It's about showing up for readers who may never sit across from you in your office, yet may feel comforted or inspired by your words.

You've already seen other therapists do this. They didn't wait for permission. They wrote from their experience, their practice, and their authentic voice. In doing so, they not only built their own credibility but also elevated the profession as a whole.

So, what's holding you back? Maybe it's fear. Maybe you think no one wants to hear your perspective, or that someone else has already said it better. But no one has lived your life, with your exact experiences, insights, and words. The most influential books are often written not by those who felt fully ready, but by those who knew their message mattered anyway.

Key Takeaways

- A book helps people get to know you before they ever meet you.

- It sets you apart and shows what you truly stand for.

- Readers who connect with your words are far more likely to become your clients.

- Writing a book is one of the simplest ways to build absolute trust—at scale.

You became a therapist to help people. Writing a book doesn't change that, it multiplies it. One hour of therapy can change one life. One book can change thousands.

You already have the knowledge. You already hold the insight. All that's left is to shape it into something others can hold in their hands and say, *"This is exactly what I needed."*

The world is waiting for more grounded, honest, and compassionate voices—your voice. So, let's turn your experience into influence. Let's turn your knowledge into a story. Let's turn your practice into a platform.

It's time to write your book.

Chapter 2

EXPANDING YOUR PROFESSIONAL NETWORK

"If you want to go fast, go alone. If you want to go far, go with others."

—— **African Proverb**

Think back to the last conference or professional meeting you attended. You may have been sitting in a crowded room with a notebook on your lap, a name tag pinned to your shirt, and a spark of curiosity in your mind. The presenter at the front held everyone's attention—not only because of what they said, but because of who they were. You may have found yourself wondering: *How did they get up there? What makes them stand out?*

Have you ever felt like just another face in the crowd at a networking event? Not because you lack knowledge or accomplishments, but because you didn't have something tangible that spoke for you—something that clearly defined your expertise, your voice, and your narrative. Sometimes, being good at what you do isn't enough in a room full of other professionals. You need something that represents you before you even say a word.

Writing a book is one of the most impactful ways to share yourself with the world. It is more than just putting your name in print. A book becomes proof of your commitment, a calling card that elevates you far beyond what a business card or résumé could ever accomplish.

It says, *"I put in the work. I developed the message. I'm ready to share it."* And when people hear that, they listen differently. They lean in. They remember. Writing a book is empowering. It can inspire you, reveal new possibilities, and show you the full power of your voice and ideas.

This chapter will show you how writing a book elevates you in your profession, not only as a therapist but as a thought leader in your field. You'll see how becoming an author raises your stature, expands your network of colleagues, and transforms everyday conversations into new and ongoing opportunities.

When I think about the professionals who regularly speak at industry events, a pattern emerges: most of them have written a book. Some also have significant media presence. Many have both. A book creates exposure, exposure builds visibility, and visibility translates into credibility. Credibility strengthens your network and, in turn, generates speaking invitations, interviews, partnerships, and published articles. In other words, one book can become the foundation for meaningful public exposure that continues to expand over time.

A strong professional network is valuable in any career. But in therapy, where human connection is at the core of the work and where new theories and techniques constantly emerge, it's absolutely essential. Staying connected with colleagues, psychologists, and mental health experts isn't just helpful; it's critical for your growth and relevance. The question is: how do you build those relationships?

One highly effective way is by publishing a book.

Writing and networking are deeply interconnected. A strong network amplifies your voice as an author, while a powerful book strengthens and expands your network. Together, they create a virtuous cycle of boosting your visibility, authority, and long-term career opportunities.

Networking Opportunities

One of the most effective ways your book can support your professional journey is by creating new connections.

> *"If opportunity doesn't knock, build a door."*
> — **Milton Berle**

Your book is a gateway to new opportunities. Picture yourself in a room with peers, leaders, and experts in your field. What's the best way to leave a lasting impression? How do you spark engagement and make an impact that goes beyond introductions? The answer is simple: hand them a copy of your book, your lasting intellectual property. Long after the event is over, your book will continue to speak on your behalf. It will carry your name, your authority, your ideas, and your values.

At professional events such as seminars, workshops, or conferences, your book becomes more than just a discussion point. It becomes a catalyst for conversations. It helps break the ice, opening the door to deeper, more meaningful exchanges with colleagues, mentors, and potential collaborators. A book not only demonstrates your value but also draws people toward you, eager to connect, exchange ideas, and explore possible partnerships. In many cases, being a published author even grants you access to exclusive gatherings, closed meetings, and expert forums that are otherwise out of reach.

And beyond in-person networking, online platforms provide a powerful way to amplify the visibility of your book. Sharing your work digitally ensures that your ideas, insights, and expertise can travel even further—reaching peers and professionals across the globe.

How to Use Your Book as a Networking Tool

Here are several effective ways to actively use your book to expand your professional relationships and presence:

- **LinkedIn**: Share excerpts, insights, or client-friendly takeaways from your book, and tag relevant people or organizations to spark engagement.

- **Email**: Include a reference to your book in your email signature, or, when appropriate, attach a sample chapter in PDF format as a helpful resource.

- **Conferences & Seminars**: Bring hard copies with you to exchange or give as thoughtful gifts. You can also reference your book in casual networking conversations or mention it during Q&A sessions to reinforce your expertise.

- **During Podcast Pitches**: Frame your book topic as the hook: "Would your listeners find value in a conversation about [your book topic]?"

- **In Direct Messages**: Use excerpts as a soft introduction to your therapeutic approach before proposing collaboration.

Using your book as a networking tool allows you to build a digital presence rooted in expertise, a quality that naturally attracts both clients and colleagues. By strategically sharing your book in online communities for therapists, patients, or professional discussion groups, you increase its reach.

As peers recommend it to their clients or colleagues, your visibility and reputation grow organically.

Becoming an author also changes the way others connect with you. The process of writing and promoting your book creates numerous opportunities to interact with experts and peers, many of which can evolve into meaningful collaborations. As a published therapist, your book instantly elevates your credibility, visibility, and authority. It becomes one of your most valuable assets: not only a way to share your knowledge, but also a gateway to new opportunities and relationships.

That said, writing and publishing a book is not without its challenges. It requires dedication, time management, and resilience in the face of rejection. But for those willing to embrace the process, authorship can be a transformative opportunity—one that amplifies your impact, strengthens your professional standing, and unlocks doors that would otherwise remain closed.

Case Study: Nedra Glover Tawwab

The professional journey of Nedra Tawwab embodies the idea of authorship. With 15 years of practice and related experience as a therapist and social worker in relationships and boundaries, she was already doing well professionally. However, in 2021, she made a dramatic shift in her career when she authored her first book, *Set Boundaries, Find Peace: A Guide to Reclaiming Yourself*.  The book, which was based on her experiential and research knowledge, was well-received by practitioners and the general audience alike. Her professional network expanded, and her future professional opportunities expanded significantly.

This book is a prime example of how authorship could elevate you professionally and open doors you never even knew existed. The book was immediately a New York Times Bestseller. People connected with the book because she approached regular real-life problems of boundaries in an emotionally intelligent, direct, and approachable way. Nedra's main point? The impact that boundaries and assertiveness have on our relationships is significant. She wanted to support people in forming healthy relationships with themselves and others.

Following the release of her book, Nedra built an audience of more than 1.8 million followers on Instagram. Her growing influence opened doors to appearances on major global platforms, including *Good Morning America*, *Red Table Talk*, and *The Breakfast Club*. The success of her book also led to the creation of a companion workbook designed to help readers apply her insights more deeply. In addition, she partnered with global brands such as Facebook, Walmart, eHarmony, Free People, and *Essence*, expanding her reach and impact even further. More recently, she followed up with another bestselling book, *Dream Free*.

Her book did more than raise her public profile—it became the gateway to a powerful professional network. It unlocked opportunities far beyond private practice, leading to media collaborations, brand partnerships, and international speaking invitations. Ultimately, it positioned Nedra as a trusted voice in her field: respected, recognizable, and in demand.

Perks of Networking

The act of writing, publishing, and promoting a book opens the door to a broader audience—both within your discipline and beyond it. Authorship, promotion, and networking work hand in hand to raise visibility and strengthen authority. As your visibility grows, so do your professional relationships, expanding your connections to colleagues, organizations, media outlets, and collaborative opportunities.

There are numerous personal and professional benefits to combining networking with authorship. Let's look at some of the key advantages:

- **Invitations to Speak at Conferences and Seminars**

Once your book is published and shared within your network, securing speaking opportunities becomes much easier. Committees organizing seminars and conferences are always on the lookout for experts who can attract an audience and provide valuable insights. Publication enhances your credibility, giving you a platform that extends well beyond your immediate practice. Speaking engagements then become a natural extension of your authorship, allowing you to share your ideas publicly, reach larger audiences, and further solidify your reputation as an authority.

A strong professional network not only enhances your visibility among peers but also raises the level of trust potential clients place in you. This credibility can increase your value as a speaker and position you for more high-profile opportunities. When peers respect your reputation, they are more likely to recommend you as an expert. Similarly, event organizers who recognize your authority and influence will be more inclined to reach out and collaborate.

Case Study: Brené Brown

Consider the case of Brené Brown, a professor at the University of Houston, and how the publication of her book transformed her life and career. Brené earned her bachelor's, master's, and Ph.D. in social work and spent more than two decades studying shame, courage, vulnerability, and empathy—topics that, for years, were largely confined to academic journals and classrooms.

Without authorship, she could have continued along the traditional path, advancing as one professor among many. What changed the trajectory of her life was the book she wrote. In 2004, she self-published her first book, titled *Women and Shame: Reaching Out, Speaking Truths, and Building Connections*. The book gained momentum, albeit slowly, and was eventually picked up by Penguin Books, which republished it as *I Thought It Was Just Me (But it isn't)* in 2007. The book laid the groundwork for her research on vulnerability and shame, but it was *The Gifts of Imperfection* (2010) that became a turning point in her public and professional life. With its simple language and emotional depth, the book became a huge hit, resonating with therapists, clients, and general readers alike. It soared to the New York Times Bestseller list, and Brené later went on to publish five other number-one New York Times bestsellers: Daring Greatly, Rising Strong, Braving the Wilderness, Dare to Lead, and Atlas of the Heart.

After her breakthrough as an author, Brené Brown was invited to countless speaking engagements, including TED Talks. Her talk *"The Power of Vulnerability"* became one of the five most viewed TED Talks of all time. In it, she distilled a decade of research on shame and vulnerability, and the talk went viral almost overnight, expanding her reach to a global audience. In 2012, she followed with *"Listening to Shame,"* which proved just as impactful Her influence grew well beyond academia. She starred in the Netflix documentary *The Call to Courage*, where she explored what it means to choose courage over comfort in today's world. She became a sought-after speaker at major corporations such as Google and Disney. She also launched two highly popular podcasts: *Unlocking Us*, a mix of interviews and solo episodes where she shares personal stories and research insights, and *Dare to Lead*, which focuses on leadership and workplace culture.

Brené also became CEO of *The Daring Way*, a professional training and certification program centered on empathy, shame, vulnerability, and courage. In 2022, HBO Max released her five-part documentary series *Brené Brown: Atlas of the Heart*, further cementing her reputation as a thought leader and cultural voice.

Brené Brown's journey—from professor to bestselling author, from researcher to global thought leader and CEO—is both remarkable and inspiring. Her visibility as an author was the catalyst. Each book brought her into contact with new people, strengthened her credibility, and opened doors that had once seemed permanently closed. Toastmasters, seminars, podcasts, corporate conferences—her network kept expanding, and that network propelled her career to new heights.

> **Unexpected Connections That Often Come from Publishing Your Book**
>
> Beyond traditional networking, publishing a book can open doors to surprising and valuable professional relationships. Authors frequently encounter opportunities like these:
>
> - Former teachers or students reaching out to reconnect or collaborate.
>
> - Invitations to guest lecture at clinical training programs or graduate classes.

- LinkedIn messages from colleagues interested in adapting your tools to their own practice or suggesting new collaborations.

- Referrals across disciplines from wellness influencers, coaches, or educators.

- Requests to co-develop webinars, courses, or other educational resources inspired by your book.

These unexpected connections not only broaden your professional reach but also strengthen your reputation as a respected and trusted voice in your field.

Collaborative Ventures

Having both a strong professional network and the credibility of being a published author significantly increases your chances of collaboration and business growth. These collaborations might take the form of co-authorship on publications, formal partnerships, or joint business initiatives. When you have established yourself as an "expert" and recognized authority in your field, you bring credibility and value to any collaboration, making others more likely to approach you for joint opportunities.

For example, if you are setting up a multi-specialty practice or planning to share office space, it becomes especially important to cultivate and maintain professional relationships with colleagues.

A well-developed network not only makes such ventures possible but also ensures that you are aligned with trusted, capable partners.

Ultimately, successful joint ventures depend on partners who share your vision and values, and those relationships are most often built through a strong, intentional professional network.

Co-Authoring Projects & Launching Joint Ventures

After Brené Brown's rise to prominence as a highly published author and well-regarded speaker, she was offered numerous collaboration opportunities. One was from Tarana Burke, an American activist and founder of the #MeToo movement. The two collaborated on the book *"You Are Your Best Thing: Vulnerability, Shame, Resilience, and the Black Experience,"* an anthology from an active community of Black writers, organizers, artists, academics, and cultural figures. The book was also a New York Times Bestseller.

The Trauma Research Foundation (TRF), co-founded by Dr. Bessel van der Kolk and Licia Sky, is a powerful example of what can happen when clinicians and researchers collaborate around a shared purpose. Following the success of *The Body Keeps the Score* and his decades of trauma research, Dr. van der Kolk recognized the need for a multidisciplinary organization that could bridge trauma science, clinical practice, and public education. Rather than working in isolation, he partnered with therapists, psychiatrists, neuroscientists, and educators to establish TRF.

Today, the foundation engages in research, training, and partnerships with a wide range of organizations to deepen our understanding of mental health and trauma recovery. While his book opened many doors and touched millions of lives, it was his collaboration with others that transformed his work into a larger movement—one with the potential for lasting global impact.

He could not have achieved this scale of impact without that book. It played a key role in establishing his credentials and building a broad audience of experts and general readers. It was that audience exposure that brought like-minded people to him and provided them with some degree of confidence and trust in the reliability and authority he would convey in proposing his foundation idea.

Increasing Referrals and Recommendations

As a therapist, you often refer patients to trusted colleagues—whether based on the patient's needs, your own availability, or geographic location. Building a strong network of peers who respect your skills and value your expertise increases the likelihood that they, in turn, will refer clients to you. Word-of-mouth referrals remain one of the most powerful ways to grow a practice.

A well-positioned book can amplify this process by boosting both your visibility and credibility. When peers read your book and connect with your perspective, they are more likely to reach out—and more inclined to refer patients to you. In this way, your book becomes not just a tool for clients but also a catalyst for professional referrals and long-term trust within your field.

Let us take an example of a doctor who is treating a patient for anxiety. The doctor recalls reading a book by a therapist about creative ways to treat anxiety. The doctor respects the author and refers the patient to the therapist. This example highlights the potential power of writing a book to build authority, as well as referrals and professional trust.

A real-life example is Dr. Dan Siegel, a psychiatrist and clinical professor at UCLA. He has brought remarkable changes to psychotherapy with his pioneering work in interpersonal neurobiology, a multidisciplinary approach that links mind, brain, and relationships. His book, *The Developing Mind*, is considered a foundational text not only for therapists but also for neuroscientists, educators, and medical professionals, and is currently in its third edition.

The popularity of his books has firmly established him as a leading figure in the field. Over the course of his career, he has authored sixteen works on mental health and related topics, several of which—such as *Mind: A Journey to the Heart of Being Human* and *Aware: The Science and Practice of Presence*—have become *New York Times* bestsellers. His growing visibility has opened doors to numerous invitations to co-create programs and workshops, allowing him to work across disciplines with professionals in mental health, neuroscience, education, healthcare, law, and beyond.

Dr. Siegel's influence has reached global leaders and institutions alike. He has consulted with the King of Thailand, Pope John Paul II, His Holiness the Dalai Lama, Google University, and the Royal Society of Arts (RSA) in London.

His books have been translated into multiple languages, and his frameworks are regularly cited by therapists and organizations worldwide. Many confidently refer clients to his programs, integrate his teachings into their own practices, and actively seek opportunities to collaborate with him.

From serving as a reference text for others to becoming a sought-after authority, Dr. Siegel has built a reputation that is both academically rigorous and practically applicable. That is the power of authorship combined with connection. Through his work, he has cultivated networks across the globe, and because of his proven expertise, peers and organizations recommend him with confidence.

Media and PR Opportunities

In today's world, where mental health is increasingly prominent and openly discussed, positioning yourself as an expert has never been more important. Recognition as an authority not only attracts more clients but also creates opportunities for professional acknowledgment and media visibility. Having a published book in your name can dramatically elevate your authority. It's often ten times easier to secure media coverage with a book than without one.

But media coverage isn't the only path to recognition. In the digital age, podcasts, webinars, online summits, blogs, and social media collaborations are among the most powerful tools for building visibility.

Nedra Tawwab is a strong example of how social media can amplify professional influence. Through consistent posting and engaging reels, she has grown her audience to an extraordinary 1.8 million followers. By sharing snippets from her book and memorable quotes, she continues to build trust and connection with potential clients in real time.

Now imagine this in your own career. You have a unique insight into a mental health issue, backed by case studies and outcomes (shared with confidentiality, of course). You publish a book around those insights. Once released, your PR team can pitch it to media outlets, educational platforms, or therapy networks. Mental health journalists and wellness publications are always looking for expert voices with clear frameworks. Every feature, interview, or article mentioning your work amplifies your credibility—transforming you from a skilled clinician into a thought leader and contributor to the wider field.

In this way, your book becomes much more than a publication. It becomes your calling card, your entry into influence, and the foundation for future interviews. It's the spark that leads to peer recommendations, conference invitations, article features, and panel appearances.

Advantages of a Professional Network

You've now reached the point where your book is published and you're beginning to build robust professional connections through it. The benefits of an expanded network go far beyond visibility and referrals. Many of them are deeply personal in nature:

- **Learning & Sharing Knowledge**: A strong network provides easier access to new ideas and exposure to innovative techniques, theories, and tools. You'll find it simpler to stay updated on industry trends, research opportunities, and best practices—and you'll have trusted colleagues to seek feedback from when navigating complex cases with discretion.

- **Emotional & Professional Support**: The work of a therapist can be incredibly demanding. Connecting with peers who face similar challenges, such as burnout or compassion fatigue, helps ease feelings of isolation and makes the struggles of the profession more manageable.

- **Mentorship**: A larger network means greater access to mentors—experts who have walked the same path. They can provide guidance on legal or ethical dilemmas, career transitions, launching a private practice, or even writing your own book.

If you're a therapist looking to grow in your career and serve more people, expanding your professional network is essential—and writing a book can be your catalyst. Many of the most trusted voices in the field didn't wait for opportunities to arrive; they created visibility by sharing their message through authorship.

Now it's your turn to step into visibility and extend your professional reach through your book.

Key Takeaways

- A book makes you visible—even when you're not in the room.

- Authorship builds influence and attracts professional connections.

- A published book leads to more speaking invitations, referrals, and collaborations.

- Your book becomes a conversation starter, a trust builder, and a lasting impression.

- Visibility through authorship fuels a stronger, more valuable network.

A book showcases your expertise and invites others into your world, helping them understand your values and why your voice matters. When clients, colleagues, and collaborators feel that clarity and confidence, they will reach out.

The next chapter will explore how authorship can strengthen your relationship with clients by deepening trust, clarifying your approach, and extending your impact.

Chapter 3

Enhancing Client Relationships

"I have come to realize that being trustworthy does not demand that I be rigidly consistent but that I be dependably real."

— **Carl Rogers**

What if your relationship with a client began before the very first session—before they filled out an intake form, drafted a nervous email, or even decided to reach out? For many therapists who have written books, this is exactly what happens. Their words are already doing the work, serving as an introduction to their voice, values, and therapeutic style long before a client steps into the room.

In those tentative early moments—when someone is still questioning whether therapy is right for them—a book can feel like a steady hand. It demystifies the process. It softens fear. It reassures them that the person on the other side is thoughtful, grounded, and capable of understanding the weight they have been carrying.

For many clients, that reassurance makes the difference between never making the call... and showing up. For therapists, it creates the foundation of a relationship built on early trust and emotional safety.

Together, they wrote *Both Sides of the Couch*—an honest, powerful account of their therapeutic journey. More than a memoir or case study, the book offered a rare dual perspective: the experiences of both the patient and the therapist. It became a bridge between their worlds.

For Anna, the book represented the continuation of her healing. For Paddy, it became a way to reach others who were suffering in silence. And for new clients, it served as a preview—an intimate window into the therapy process and into Paddy himself: his character, his professionalism, and his clinical approach. Readers arrived at their first session already familiar with his style, which 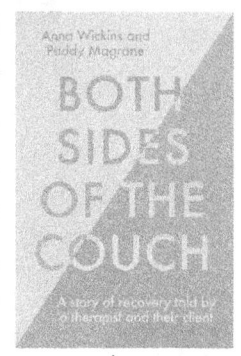 made their conversations more focused from the very beginning. The book helped Paddy establish trust and confidence with his clients before they even entered the room.

Their story underscores a core truth: the client–therapist relationship is paramount. More than degrees, titles, or years of experience, what matters most is how you communicate—and the trust you are able to build.

In the field of therapy, few have had as profound an influence on the profession as Carl Rogers. He is the founder of person-centered therapy, meaning that Rogers elevated our understanding of the therapeutic relationship to determine what constitutes healing. In his book *On Becoming a Person,* Rogers offered a new understanding of meaningful change in therapy.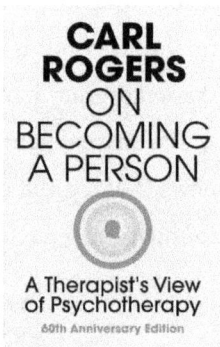

He emphasized authentic communication, deep empathy, and unconditional positive regard as key elements of change, rather than techniques and diagnoses. Rogers' writing and insights did not just resonate with therapists—his ability to articulate empathy and emotional safety helped clients feel seen and understood, often for the first time. He demonstrated that therapeutic connection could begin long before a client sat down in the room.

This idea remains just as powerful today. Just as Rogers used the written word to extend empathy, clarity, and trust beyond the session, you can do the same. A well-written book allows you to introduce your voice and values to clients before therapy begins. Your words can act as a first point of connection, offering reassurance, demystifying the process, and building emotional safety from the start.

This chapter explores how writing a book can enhance the therapeutic relationship between a therapist and their client. Yes, a book can be a marketing/networking vehicle, but it primarily serves as a significant communication tool, not just a form. A book can be a way to respond to a client who needs understanding, reassurance, and hope. A book creates a connection, builds trust, and clarifies your work and its purpose. When someone thinks they have been understood before a word is uttered, there is a greater chance of connecting and confidence in the therapist to take them through the therapeutic work. Overall, this makes therapy much easier on the client.

Writing is an extension of the therapeutic relationship. As you use your voice to facilitate clients in the room, your words on the page also provide clarity, empathy, and support outside of the room.

Improving Communication Through Your Book

Your book has the potential to enhance communication with clients by making therapy more explicit, reassuring clients in times of confusion, and setting specific expectations. Here are some concrete approaches it is helpful in the therapy process:

- **Educating and Empowering Clients:** Many clients often feel uncertain or confused during the initial stages of therapy. They may also have difficulty understanding the structure or expectations of the process when attending their first sessions. They come in with a mix of anxiety and skepticism. As a therapist, how do you manage this situation? Consider writing a book. The beauty of a book is its ability to provide clarity around the therapeutic experience. Many people read self-help books and guides to understand concepts of psychology, and these elements of clarity can be made more transparent through precise language, relatable metaphors, examples, and case studies. For example, a client may be very anxious and then read your book. Your book could explain what anxiety is, discuss its causes and symptoms, and depict how you have been helpful in those moments. Writing can both help clients understand their circumstances and manage anxiety and feelings of isolation. A book can also provide familiarity with you, including your knowledge, tone of voice, and style of therapy, allowing you to build a relationship of trust. So, if clients read your book before or between sessions, they can arrive at that session better prepared.

At times, a single therapy session may not be sufficient for both you and your client. As a therapist, you may face a challenge in remaining closely engaged in the client's healing journey, and they may feel hesitant to call you every time they have doubts or questions. This is where your book becomes valuable. It can take the form of a self-help guide or a collection of FAQs.

Your book can communicate on your behalf, even after the session. The book enables clients to reflect on their thoughts and insights, thereby maintaining the therapeutic relationship. When clients read your book, they stay connected to your voice, engaging with your therapeutic perspective, guiding principles, and insights. This helps maintain the continuity of the relationship between sessions. The client can feel heard and have their uncertainties addressed, while also eliminating any misgivings.

A book allows you to respond to client fears with clarity and empathy. As they read, they begin forming a connection with your voice and worldview. They come to understand your perspective on healing, your relational style, and your approach to client problems. This connection helps lessen anxiety, encourages better participation before sessions, and lowers dropout rates. Clients who have read your book before starting with you appear to open up faster and are more likely to attend therapy or remain committed to therapy goals. When you write in clear, kind, and empathetic terms and make your own experiences accessible to clients, you create a map for their healing process. You expand the therapeutic relationship and establish a lasting connection of trust, guidance, and emotional safety.

Case study: Lori Gottlieb and *Maybe You Should Talk to Someone*

We mentioned Lori Gottlieb in the first chapter, but her work is especially worth revisiting here for its effective strengthening of the client-therapist connection beyond the session. She had shared true stories from her practice, along with her own experiences, in her *New York Times* bestselling book, *Maybe You Should Talk to Someone: A Therapist, Her Therapist, and Our Lives Revealed*. 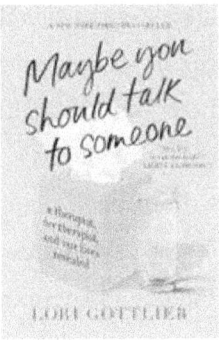 The book is a reflection of two worlds: Lori, both as a therapist and someone receiving therapy.

Through her uncomplicated, story-centered approach, she articulated psychological concepts like grief, denial, and transference in ways that speak to readers emotionally. She incorporated internal questions that clients often feel too timid to ask, and helped to turn her book into a method of education and healing. Many reviewers noted the book's candor and rawness as truly valuable. Many readers have shared that reading the book helped them to learn how therapy works and what to expect. Many clients reported that the book was the impetus for them to seek help as well. To help increase the power of clients' comfort and hopefulness heading into their first session, many therapists have since deemed the book a worthwhile recommendation as pre-therapy reading.

- **Using Books to Address Common Concerns:** In addition to letting clients know about therapy in general, your book can also address more specific concerns. When writing a book, it is essential to recognize the roles of your readers.

You can do this by considering the client's perspective and imagining the questions or concerns they may have. A Frequently Asked Questions section can help save time for you while also educating and empowering your clients. It saves you time by addressing common concerns and frequently asked questions, providing a level of reassurance before clients walk in the door. An FAQ section provides a "quick" and readily available information source, while establishing some level of trust and understanding before they even enter into the psychotherapy process.

Book Formats That Work Well in Therapy

Not every therapist's book has to be a full memoir, academic text, or a frequently asked questions book. Other valid formats that might strengthen your client interactions are as follows:

- **Client handbook:** It will provide an overview of your approach, philosophy, and process for new clients.

- **Session Companion Guide**: This can include exercises, journaling prompts, or reflection points tied to the session topics. Such guides will improve client engagement.

- **Post-therapy integration guide:** This will be helpful to clients as they transition out of active therapy.

- **Mini-topic guides:** Information that is specific to niche topics, such as trauma grounding, boundary setting, or sleep hygiene.

- **Your Book as a Consistent Source of Support:** A thoughtfully designed book is a dependable and silent partner for your clients—a source of support they can consult whenever they wish. This will help patients feel less isolated during moments of doubt or difficulty and will also encourage them to reflect more deeply on their recovery, becoming more present in the healing process. It encourages independence while also solidifying the trust and safety of the therapeutic relationship, even outside of sessions.

How One Therapist Could Make a Book Part of Every Client's Journey

To illustrate how therapists might incorporate books into their clinical work, let's consider a fictional example that draws on real-world techniques.

Dr. Amina Joshi, a relational trauma specialist (fictional for this example), gives every new client a short e-book titled *Before We Begin: A Gentle Guide to Trauma Therapy*. While Dr. Joshi herself is not a real practitioner, the approach described is based on strategies commonly used by therapists to enhance client engagement and improve outcomes.

This is how it could work:
- Before intake, a welcome email is sent to clients, accompanied by an eBook that provides an overview of Dr. Joshi's therapeutic model and what to expect during therapy.

> - Between sessions, clients are assigned chapters from the book as optional reading to prepare them for further reflecting on the topics shared in therapy.
>
> - During sessions, responses to the book serve as starting points for more in-depth discussions, helping clients express thoughts they might not otherwise have.
>
> - After the session, the book is kept by the clients as a self-guided reference tool to help them after they leave therapy.
>
> This structured use of a book demonstrates how written material can extend the therapeutic alliance beyond the session. It becomes a silent partner, supporting, educating, and connecting clients to their healing journey.

Building Trust and Loyalty
- **Demonstrating Transparency:** Trust is one of the most valuable currencies in any therapeutic relationship—especially since therapy so often involves emotional uncertainty and vulnerability. A book can help establish a loyal and trusting connection with patients by demonstrating professional competence, openness in practice, and a genuine commitment to those you serve.

Writing a book is no small undertaking. It requires a significant investment of time, energy, and often money. Yet that investment is also a promise—to uphold your values, honor your experience, and serve your clients with integrity. In many ways, your book becomes a narrative of your journey: the obstacles you've faced, the lessons you've learned, and the insights you've gained along the way. This act of openness is an exercise in both authenticity and leadership.

By sharing your professional story, along with carefully chosen personal experiences and illustrative examples from your life or clinical work (always protecting confidentiality), you allow clients to see *you*. They see your authentic self and your professional stance. That early connection helps ease hesitation and lays the groundwork for a trusting therapeutic relationship before the first session even begins.

- **Establishing Authority and Warmth:** A book is also one of the most effective ways to establish authority in your field and strengthen your personal brand. It allows you to demonstrate your expertise by presenting your knowledge, ideas, and clinical insights in a lasting, structured format. Unlike fleeting online posts or casual conversations, a book provides a permanent record of your professional perspective and approach.

At the same time, a book communicates warmth. The way you frame your insights and stories makes your expertise approachable, allowing readers to feel both reassured by your authority and connected to your humanity. This combination of authority and warmth is what inspires trust, loyalty, and long-term relationships.

However, the authority is not built by asserting superiority, but by embodying authenticity. Take, for example, psychotherapist Joshua Fletcher. In his book *And How Does That Make You Feel?*, he opens the door to his thoughts as a therapist during his sessions with patients dealing with anxiety. In sharing moments of self-doubt, embarrassment, and overwhelm, Fletcher became a deeply empathetic and relatable figure. Readers not only gained a glimpse of his clinical insight but also saw how he navigates his challenges. This humanizes the therapist and helps clients feel less judged, more understood, and emotionally safer. They will put their trust and loyalty in the therapist's capability precisely because they have already witnessed your resilience and approach through your book.

- **Reinforcing Consistency:** When I talk about consistency in therapy, I don't mean superficial things, like wearing the same clothes every session (as some therapists do). I mean consistently showing up in alignment with your words, tone, and presence. When words do not match your actions, clients may perceive you as inconsistent or untrustworthy. In therapy, consistency is an essential factor in establishing trust, and it reinforces that trust when what you have in black and white <-> written work, reflects the subject matter and intended meanings discussed in a therapy session. In the absence of presence or absence in a therapy session, the book will always be there to provide scaffolding for their ideas and establish a consistency of practice that intersects with what they hear in the moment.

When the advice people are reading intersects with what they hear, clients feel more confident in your method, and you reassure them. In addition to reinforcing trust, consistency enables customers to integrate essential ideas over time.

- **Enhancing Relationships Beyond the Client:** Clients are not the only ones affected by mental health challenges. Families, caregivers, and community leaders also benefit from understanding the therapeutic process and recognizing their role in it.

Beyond helping potential clients and establishing credibility among peers, writing a book can also deepen stakeholder engagement. A well-written book can help those around the client better understand the issues, what patients may be experiencing, and how they can play a meaningful part in the healing journey.

A compelling real-world example comes from a mixed-methods study published in *Frontiers in Psychiatry* that examined how a picture book supported caregivers of children with autism spectrum disorder. The study, informed by interviews, field observations, and input from multiple disciplines, distributed the book to 54 families. Results showed significant reductions in caregiver stress. In their feedback, families described the book as warm, inspiring, and helpful in making sense of their family dynamics and in expanding their understanding of autism. Many even expressed a desire to share the book more widely, underscoring how therapist-created tools can educate and emotionally support a client's entire circle.

By engaging caregivers in this way, the book transformed them from passive observers into active participants in therapy.

They became more aware, more empathetic, and better able to support their loved ones. When you integrate tools like this into your practice, you foster empathy, reduce isolation, and promote shared understanding within care networks—benefiting not only the client, but the entire community of care.

- **Measuring the Impact of Your Book:** Although a book can sometimes feel like a one-way conversation, it can also become an integral part of the therapeutic experience. When written with care and intention, your book can spark ongoing dialogue, surface client needs, and inform the next stage of your work. Observing how clients engage with your writing provides insights into their reflections, emotional states, and recurring themes—often revealing more than an intake form or a casual conversation ever could.

- **Feedback Loops:** When you, as the therapist, actively gather and reflect on client feedback, your book becomes an interactive extension of therapy. Clients may arrive at sessions with new thoughts or emotions stirred by what they've read, leading to deeper and more substantive conversations. For some, encountering your words outside the session helps clarify feelings or gives them practice articulating thoughts they may have struggled to say aloud. This interaction can serve as a catalyst for self-reflection and more meaningful dialogue in the room.

- **Tracking Engagement:** Understanding how clients connect with your content offers valuable insights. By incorporating prompts—such as journaling exercises, reflection questions, or worksheets—you gain a clearer sense of what resonates most. Whether clients complete a reflective activity, watch a video you've linked, or engage with a guided practice before a session, these layers enrich therapy and give you measurable feedback. Over time, they also help guide the creation of future resources tailored to clients' needs.

While intake forms or static websites provide basic information, a book creates something much more personal. It introduces clients to your tone, philosophy, and thoughtfulness before they ever walk through the door. That sense of care can be powerful. Clients feel seen before they've spoken a word.

For therapists, this means that clients arrive with less hesitation and more openness. They enter sessions not just informed, but already beginning to trust. In many ways, your book does some of the emotional heavy lifting, laying the foundation for connection, safety, and shared direction.

Whether it educates, offers comfort, tells your story, or clarifies your approach, your book becomes more than content—it becomes a steady presence clients can return to again and again. It reflects the heart of your work and carries your voice beyond the walls of your practice. In a profession where relationships are everything, your words can serve as a companion in your clients' journeys, quietly reinforcing what's possible even in your absence.

You don't need to be a bestselling author. You don't need to have all the answers. What matters is showing up on the page with the same care, clarity, and intention you bring into the room. That alone makes your book powerful.

Key Takeaways
- A well-crafted book strengthens client connection through clear communication, establishes trust, and demonstrates your commitment.

- Your book can serve as a bridge between sessions, a reflection of your values, and an avenue for broader engagement.

- Writing with intention deepens both clinical impact and personal connection.

- A book can enhance stakeholder involvement and provide ways to measure the impact of your therapeutic techniques.

As a therapist, your presence is your most powerful tool—and your words can extend that presence beyond the therapy room. By putting your voice into a book, you create something lasting: a source of clarity, reassurance, and guidance that clients can return to again and again.

In the next chapter, we'll explore how you can build on this foundation of trust to foster stronger client outcomes—and expand your influence far beyond the one-on-one session.

Chapter 4

Boosting Your Therapy Practice's Reputation

"There's nothing in our culture that credentials you quite like a published book."

—— **Michael Hyatt**

What if your next client came to you—not through a flyer or social media ad, but because they read your book and felt you already understood them?

Imagine the transformative power of your words. At 2 a.m., someone picks up your book searching for relief—and in its pages, they feel seen. That is the hidden power of authorship. A book doesn't just explain *how* you work; it communicates your voice, your values, and builds trust long before you ever meet the client. This is the power you hold in your hands.

In a world flooded with marketing noise, a well-written book becomes your clearest signal. It positions you as an expert, amplifies your message, and creates opportunities you might never have imagined—media coverage, speaking invitations, deeper client relationships, and long-term credibility.

For many therapists, authorship has been more than a marketing tool; it has been a turning point. Their books didn't just promote services—they sparked movements, challenged stigma, and created lasting impact.

So, what's stopping you?

When Dr. Edith Eger decided to pour her life as a Holocaust survivor into words, she didn't know how vastly it would change the lives of many, the impact it would create on the world, and, importantly, how much it would alter the trajectory of her career. Her 2017 book, *The Choice: Embrace the Possible*, explores the challenges of healing and the complex emotions tied to trauma and survivor's guilt.

The book was a New York Times and Sunday Times bestseller, boosting her professional influence and earning her invitations to speak at universities, mental health conferences, and media outlets worldwide. Once her book was published, Dr. Eger's clinic gained significant credibility and visibility. Referrals increased, and media outlets and publishers frequently sought her out for interviews and expert commentary. Her practice soon reached peak popularity, with waitlists stretching for months.

Through her writing, Dr. Eger moved from being a respected therapist to becoming a recognized thought leader whose ideas are discussed far beyond the four walls of her office. Her book not only established her authority and credibility but also gave her practice a presence on the global stage.

Enhancing the Story of Your Practice

Your therapy practice has a special story, a combination of values, mission, and clinical approach. A book will let you exemplify and preserve that story in a lasting way. It is not just a marketing tool.

It is a record of your work and the impact you are making in the world. Your story is worth telling, and a book is the ideal format for you to do that.

Consider the example of Dr. Marsha Linehan. A clinical psychologist and researcher who has profoundly reshaped the field of mental health with the development of Dialectical Behavior Therapy (a treatment especially effective for borderline personality disorder and chronic suicidality). Even though she was already a well-known name in clinical settings, it was her memoir, *Building a Life Worth Living* (2020), that brought both her story and her work into the mainstream consciousness. In her memoir, Marsha Linehan shared her own experience with mental illness and psychiatric hospitalization—an unprecedented act of vulnerability from a clinical expert. The book significantly elevated her profile and influence, both within the therapeutic community and beyond. It also cemented her status as a pioneer in psychological treatment and as a courageous voice in the effort to de-stigmatize mental health.

Over the course of her career, Linehan has authored four books, including treatment manuals now used by clinicians worldwide. Her groundbreaking research has earned her numerous awards, among them the **Marsha Linehan Award for Outstanding Research in the Treatment of Suicidal Behavior**, established by the American Association of Suicidology. She also served as director of the Behavioral Research and Therapy Clinics and remains one of the most sought-after guides for professionals in her field.

Marketing and Branding with Your Book

In marketing, consistency is key, and a book provides a consistent, credible message that you can share everywhere your audience is.

- **Your Book as a Brand Anchor:** A book is one of the most powerful ways to define and promote your therapy practice. It captures the essence of your work—your values, approach, and methodology—and communicates that message clearly and permanently. Instead of repeating your story in every consultation call or advertisement, your book can articulate it once and for all, often more effectively than ads or conversations alone. For journalists, peers, and potential clients, a thoughtful and helpful book leaves a lasting impression. Clients are far more likely to trust and remember someone who has written a resource that speaks directly to their needs. From a marketing standpoint, it also simplifies your efforts: you now have a concrete product to promote across social media, your website, or at live events. Unlike social media posts or short-lived campaigns, a book endures.

Your book is more than a credential—it is a strategic expression of your voice, your values, and your therapeutic philosophy. Over time, it shapes how others perceive you, reinforcing your identity as both a trusted expert and practicing clinician. Positioned well, it can open doors to collaborations, workshops, speaking engagements, and media appearances. In this way, your book becomes a true anchor for your brand, extending your influence far beyond the therapy room—if that is your goal.

Dr. Catherine Steiner-Adair: Real-Life Marketing Campaign Example

As a parent and educator, Dr. Catherine Steiner-Adair published "The Big Disconnect: Protecting Childhood and Family Relationships in the Digital Age," a book that examined how excessive screen time and digital distractions were impacting children's social and emotional growth. Alongside the book, Dr. Steiner-Adair launched a companion series of blog posts that included not only anecdotal experiences but also a few helpful tips for parents. One of the blog posts, "Why Your Child Melts Down After Screen Time," went viral and was shared across numerous parenting forums and educational websites. As the buzz around the book generated, Abbie was invited to lead seminars and speak with groups of parents at schools. The book elevated Abbie's stature as a child psychology expert, but the meaningful message also led to six additional speaking engagements, media placements, and new client work.

Aligning Your Visual Brand

When publishing your book, make sure that its design and tone mirror your professional presence:

- **Book Cover:** Use the same color palette, fonts, and overall mood as your website or logo. This consistency makes your brand instantly recognizable.

- **Headshot and Bio:** Include your professional photo in the *About the Author* section—ideally the same one used on your website and other platforms.

- **Language, Style, and Tone:** Your book's voice should reflect your therapeutic personality. If you are warm and conversational in sessions, let that same voice come through in your writing. This creates a sense of familiarity for clients when they meet you.

  A cohesive brand builds trust and recognition. Ideally, your book and your website should feel aligned, so that clients experience your voice and identity consistently across every platform.

- **Leveraging Your Book to Boost Reputation:** Your book is not just a finished product—it's a living tool for engagement, trust-building, and visibility. Here are ten practical ways to use it to strengthen your reputation and expand your practice:

1. Host Webinars or Workshops – Turn your chapters or key themes into interactive sessions. For example, if your book is on anxiety, host a webinar titled *"3 Ways to Reduce Anxiety in Teens."*

2. Create Social Media Content – Share short quotes, practical tips, or mini-excerpts regularly to reach and engage your audience.

3. Offer the Book as a Lead Magnet – Provide a free chapter or digital download in exchange for email signups, building a list of genuinely interested readers.

4. Use It in Client Onboarding – Give new clients a copy (or a chapter) to introduce your approach, build trust, and prepare them for your therapy style.

5. Pitch to Media & Podcasts – Position your book as your calling card when requesting guest appearances or interviews; authors are viewed as subject-matter experts.

6. Build a Course or Program – Expand your book's core message into a paid course, group program, or coaching package, creating both impact and additional revenue.

7. Send Copies to Referral Sources – Share your book with doctors, schools, or community leaders to reinforce your credibility and keep your name top-of-mind.

8. Include It in Speaking Engagements – Offer your book as a takeaway at workshops or conferences, leaving a lasting impression.

9. Feature It in Your Email & Website – Add your book's title and URL to your email signature, and highlight it prominently on your homepage or *About* page.

10. Host Community Book Talks – Organize small discussion groups—online or in person—around your book's theme to deepen engagement and build local visibility.

Integrating Your Book into Your Local and Online Presence

Your book can strengthen your professional image across both digital and in-person platforms. Here are several ways to integrate it into the spaces where potential clients are already looking for you:

- **Professional Forums**: Create or update your profile on platforms like *Psychology Today*. List your book title in your bio, and if it addresses areas such as anxiety, trauma, or relationships, include it under "Specialties." For example: *Author of "Book Title," a guide to understanding and managing trauma.* A short, targeted description positions you as a trusted expert.

- **Google My Business (GMB)**: Post about your book in the *What's New* or *Updates* sections. Add the cover image to your photos, and link directly to the book on your website. *(Bonus: Without soliciting testimonials, you can encourage readers or colleagues to mention your book in their Google reviews.)*

- **Therapy Directories**: On sites like *GoodTherapy* or *TherapyDen*, use the "Publications" or "Credentials" section to display your book cover, description, and a short note on how it supports your practice. This immediately boosts your credibility when clients are comparing options.

- **Local Events & Libraries**: Partner with libraries, clinics, or nonprofits to host a discussion or workshop. You might also donate copies to waiting rooms in partner practices or community spaces, ensuring your book reaches people where they need it most.

- **Brand Growth and Community Building:** Publishing a book creates an asset that promotes brand expansion and deepens engagement with your community. Online book clubs, discussion groups, and live Q&A sessions give readers a chance to articulate their ideas, share reflections, and interact with others. Even if your community primarily gathers around other books, these opportunities reinforce your credibility as a subject matter expert while also building trust and loyalty.

Your credibility can grow even further through collaboration. Endorsements, co-authored chapters, and guest contributions from other subject matter experts not only elevate your visibility but also extend your reach to new audiences. These collaborations not only strengthen your reputation but also expose your work to communities you may not have otherwise reached.

Media and PR Opportunities
- **How a Book Attracts Media Attention:** Credibility is the quality or power of inspiring belief. Publishing a book is a guaranteed way to achieve it, and that credibility is precisely what media outlets and journalists seek. When they need an expert to comment on a trending topic, they often turn to those who've already demonstrated thought leadership in print. As an author, you are viewed as someone knowledgeable and able to express it effectively, which makes you a perfect guest for panels, podcasts, and interviews. A book also strengthens your press materials: it makes pitches more compelling and gives producers or editors a solid reason to feature you.

A prime example is Terrence "Terry" Real, a renowned family therapist and founder of the Relational Life Institute. He brought widespread attention to the subjects of male depression and relationships through his bestselling books *I Don't Want to Talk About It* and *Us: Getting Past You and Me to Build a More Loving Relationship*.

The credibility of his writing opened doors to major media opportunities, including features in *The New York Times* and *The Los Angeles Times*, as well as appearances on *Good Morning America* and *The Oprah Winfrey Show*. His books not only amplified his voice but also established him as a leading authority on marriage and mental health. Terry Real's story illustrates a powerful truth: a book can elevate a therapist's reputation and extend their influence far beyond the consulting room.

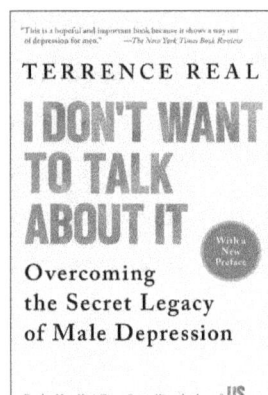

- **Becoming a Go-To Expert:** Publishing a book can make you a highly sought-after source for articles, interviews, and expert commentary. With your book in hand, you enter the conversation as an established authority in your field. Journalists and media outlets consistently look for authors who project credibility, expertise, and thought leadership—and a published book delivers all three. This exposure allows you to amplify your profession, message, and mission to a much wider audience.

Authority also opens doors to speaking engagements, panel invitations, and conference presentations. These opportunities expand your reach, strengthen professional connections, and position you for collaborations with peers, partners, and future clients. Each interview or media appearance not only builds awareness but also drives people to your website and social platforms, creating a steady flow of visibility and trust.

In a crowded marketplace, few tools are as powerful as a book. It signals that you are credible, relatable, and human—all qualities that attract both clients and opportunities. Writing a book is one of the most effective ways to claim that authority and ensure your voice stands out.

- **Stats or Data:** A 2006 survey, *The Business Impact of Writing a Book*, conducted with 200 authors, highlighted just how powerful authorship can be for professional growth. **96%** reported that publishing a book had a positive impact on their business—from greater visibility to stronger client relationships. **94%** said it enhanced their brand and gave them a more defined, professional image. **96%** noted that authorship increased their clientele, thanks to the instant credibility and authority a book provides. **87%** were able to raise their fees after publishing.

These numbers tell a clear story: a book doesn't just shape how others see you—it elevates your authority, boosts your confidence, and increases the perceived value of your services.

- **Using Your Book to Drive Content Marketing:** There are many ways to repurpose materials for platforms like blogs, social media, webinars, and podcasts. If you write a book, it can be a gold mine for marketing. Reusing ideas, stories, and lessons from the book helps develop a narrative that supports your brand across media. You can transform each chapter into several detailed blog posts, increasing traffic, boosting engagement, strengthening SEO, and positioning yourself as a thought leader.

Concepts from the book can also become short, shareable quotes for social media, keeping your brand visible, engaging followers, and reinforcing your message online.

Podcasts, along with webinars, serve as highly effective methods to repurpose your book content. Planning a webinar series that explores the major themes of your book gives you the chance to dive deeper into specific topics while interacting directly with participants and building a network. Broadcasting your content through podcasts enables you to reach a wider audience while establishing authority—further promoting both your book and your service offerings.

According to *Forbes*, using your book to create digital products (e.g., e-books, infographics, whitepapers) can be an excellent way to generate leads. These products provide value upfront, attract potential clients to your website, and allow you to capture their information for future marketing efforts.

Using your book to create content across multiple platforms enables you to extend your message while maintaining consistency and coherence. This increases your return on investment because your book becomes more than something to read—it becomes a foundation for a full marketing ecosystem. Repurposing also reinforces your core message and gives you a variety of engaging content to connect with your audience. It supports your brand by keeping you visible and professional across channels, helping you grow your presence and influence in the long term.

> **Enhancing Stakeholder Engagement**
> - Use your book to align and impress key stakeholders:
> - Referral sources (doctors, schools, HR departments)
> - Strategic partners (mental health orgs, insurance providers).
> - Create "value packs" with your book and related resources for partners.
> - Gift the book at stakeholder events, during business development meetings, or as part of welcome packages.

Creating a Legacy

A book will help you create an enduring legacy by conveying your knowledge, experiences, and values to future generations. It is more than just thoughts on a page—it can become a permanent representation of your life's work, encapsulating the career and wisdom you have developed throughout your journey.

If you are a psychotherapist, psychologist, or other helping professional, your book can enlighten and guide colleagues or students, while also helping your clients. It represents a legitimate contribution to the growth of your profession. Your book can be a source of inspiration, knowledge, and ideas that will carry on long after you have stopped practicing. Writing a book allows your influence to endure far beyond the work of your day-to-day practice.

Take, for example, the author and psychiatrist Dr. Irvin D. Yalom. He has written several critically acclaimed professional texts, including *The Gift of Therapy* and *Love's Executioner*—books that are studied and valued in psychotherapy training programs around the globe. Dr. Yalom has narrated fascinating case studies, provided valuable insights into therapy, and offered reflective perspectives throughout his work. Many generations of mental health professionals have benefited from his writing, which continues to inspire and educate.

Your voice does not need to end at the therapy room door. As a therapist, you change lives one conversation at a time—but when you put your ideas into the written word, they gain something more: reach, credibility, and staying power.

A book carries your thoughts farther, into more hands, and strengthens your credibility. It brings your message to places and moments you may never know—your words on someone's nightstand, in the waiting area of a doctor's office, or in the hands of a person who needs your wisdom the most. Your words do not just inform. They connect. They move. They motivate.

Key Takeaways
- A well-written book can:

- Establish yourself as an expert in your niche.

- Serve as the centerpiece of your marketing efforts.

- Open doors to media, speaking, and networking opportunities.

- Deepen your connection with clients, partners, and the public.

- Help you leave a legacy and shape your professional identity for years to come.

Writing a book is one of the most potent and personal steps you can take to shape your professional identity. It builds lasting trust, elevates your practice, and leaves behind something that continues to work long after you've left the room.

Chapter 5

Personal and Professional Fulfilment

"The desire to create is one of the deepest yearnings of the human soul."
— **Dieter F. Uchtdorf**

You've spent hours listening, holding space, and guiding others toward healing. But what happens when you realize you have a story of your own to tell?

Not just the stories you've witnessed, but the wisdom you've earned. The patterns you've seen in human suffering, the breakthroughs you've witnessed, and the insights that keep surfacing session after session—all of it starts to form something bigger.

For many therapists, the desire to write does not begin with a hope of being published. It begins with a feeling. A quiet but steadily building need to communicate an insight, provide hope, or record the experiences that shape both us and our clients. Over time, that feeling can no longer be ignored.

Writing a book then becomes something more than a professional project. It becomes a service. It becomes a witty, wise, and deeply human way of conveying public meaning from private understanding. It becomes another kind of reflection that enhances your growth as a therapist. It becomes a way of fulfilling a greater purpose: to expand your influence beyond the therapy room, to put into writing what matters most, and to create a lasting record of your voice as part of the wider healing journey.

And maybe, more than anything, it becomes a chance to finally tell the truth—in your voice, on your terms.

Psychotherapist **Rahima Warren** experienced this same calling. After years of clinical practice, she found herself drawn to fiction as a way to reflect on and explore themes of trauma, forgiveness, and transformation. Her debut novel, *The Star-Seer's Prophecy*, uses a fantasy lens, yet its core speaks to emotional healing and the depths we must sometimes face in recovery. In many ways it is fiction, but in its essence, it is truth.

Speaking about the writing process, Warren reflected:
"The process of getting the story down and perfecting it was its own reward — along with an expanded ease of being not only a writer but a good writer."

Her words remind us that the rewards of writing can be greater than overt professional recognition. Indeed, for therapist-authors, writing can serve as a form of healing for both the self and the eventual readers.

Accomplishing Personal Milestones

Many things would define completion for writing a book. For one, completing a book is an accomplishment. This accomplishment has physical, visible, and permanent proof of your knowledge, experience, and commitment. Writing a book takes discipline, focus, and commitment. Though the process can be long, few things match the sense of accomplishment that comes with finishing it.

Suppose your book is the solution someone has been looking for when they are having difficulties in their personal or professional lives — How satisfying is that idea? The process of writing a book involves growth and self-discovery. Writing becomes a profoundly fulfilling and significant act when you focus on the purpose and the influence your work can have on others.

Personal Satisfaction of Becoming a Published Author.

Writing a book is a transformative experience. It encourages deep reflection, insight, and structured expression. The process may be challenging, but it's worth the effort.

Publishing a book is like running a marathon — a testament to your persistence and dedication. Publishing your book can boost your confidence and self-esteem, reinforcing your belief in your skills and potential.

A real-life example of this transformation is Dr. Nicole LePera, also known as *The Holistic Psychologist*. She explained in interviews and radio appearances that writing her book, *How to Do the Work*, was not just a creative endeavor for her, but also a profoundly transforming event that allowed her to distill years of clinical practice, reflect on her healing journey, and reinforce her therapeutic philosophy. On The Intentional Advantage podcast, she highlighted how the book helped her clarify her vision and organize and implement her holistic model, which combines mind, body, and spirit in practice.

In her case, the outcome went beyond name recognition—her book became a platform that advanced her career. She became a thought leader in inclusive mental wellness as a result of the book's widespread media coverage and the speaking engagements it led to worldwide. Nicole's story illustrates how publishing a book can have a profound impact on both professional and personal life, as well as personal growth.

Leaving a Legacy

Not every author writes to gain fame or money. Some authors write solely for themselves or their families—and that is a valid, deeply meaningful choice. Many people feel the need to document their struggles and the lessons they've learned, hoping their readers won't have to face the same hardships. This act of sharing goes far beyond personal therapy—it is an act of service.

Senior experts from different fields are often seen writing memoirs filled with anecdotes, insights, lessons learned, and personal stories from their years of experience. For example, we at Stardom Books assisted a millionaire in publishing his life narrative, with the primary purpose of preserving the hard-won lessons of his journey in a way that would instruct and inspire others.

By preserving your knowledge, values, and experiences for future generations, your book creates a lasting legacy, one that will continue to inspire, educate, and influence people long after you are gone.

Creating a lasting impact in the field of therapy

Writing a book as a therapist enables you to contribute to the body of knowledge in your field. Your distinct viewpoints, case studies, and professional experiences can help other practitioners, raise mental health awareness among the general public, and guide best practices. In addition to shaping the future of the therapeutic field, publishing allows you to share your own narrative and voice.

A book gives you a lasting way to make an impact beyond the therapy room. It becomes a tangible reflection of your values, your beliefs about therapy, and the trajectory of your career. It also serves as a valuable resource for others—whether as a teaching instrument added to a university reading list, a reference for professional peers, or an inspiration to those seeking guidance.

As mental health stigma decreases, therapists are more valuable than ever. A book that combines not just theory and practice, but also empathy, affirmation, and hope, can become your contribution to this cultural shift. Rather than effecting change one therapeutic encounter at a time, you gain the ability to impact many.

When a therapist authors a book, authorship becomes more than a personal achievement—it becomes an act of service. You contribute to the ongoing development of your field, leave your mark and legacy, and create a meaningful impact that extends far beyond your practice.

Contributing to Therapeutic Literature and Education

Starting a book-writing project is a profoundly life-changing experience. Writing a book invites you to reflect on your experience, evaluate your growth, and deepen your understanding. Therapists who write books are part of a long tradition of mental health professionals who, with commitment, introspection, and perseverance, have made essential contributions to therapeutic literature and the larger cultural landscape.

Your writing can significantly contribute to the field of mental health. Previously discussed psychiatrist and trauma researcher Dr. Bessel van der Kolk, who authored the bestselling book *The Body Keeps the Score*, has transformed the field's understanding of trauma. His work helped the public understand the profound effects of trauma on the body and mind. It has influenced educational policy in schools and prisons,  sparked public debate, stayed on The New York Times bestseller list for years, and is still a standard recommendation among trainees and therapists.

By transforming decades of clinical research and case studies into a compelling narrative, Dr. Bessel van der Kolk has created a permanent resource that therapists, educators, and advocates continue to depend on. The growing use of therapies such as Eye Movement Desensitization and Reprocessing (EMDR), trauma-informed yoga, and somatic experiencing in professional settings is proof that his writing has had a direct influence on trauma-informed practices.

In addition to van der Kolk, many other therapist-authors—such as Lori Gottlieb (*Maybe You Should Talk to Someone*) and Irvin Yalom (*Love's Executioner*)—have demonstrated that books hold the power not only to inspire and educate, but also to reshape the way the general public understands psychological healing and rehabilitation.

Your input, too, can become a long-lasting resource—one that supports, empowers, and trains others while contributing to the ongoing advancement of the field of therapy.

Personal and Professional Growth

Dr. Prerna Kohli, the recipient of the '100 Women Achievers' award in India, is one of the most prominent clinical psychologists in the country. When talking about personal and professional development, it is worthwhile to recall her path from psychologist to author. A book was more than just ink on paper to Dr. Kohli. It was an instrument for spreading her ideas and power.

As a result of her years of experience working closely with an authority on workplace wellness, jail reform, and rehabilitation, she wrote a book called *Psychologist Musings*, which helped disseminate this information to the world. Her writing style combined professional insights with personal experiences, creating a relatable and approachable book for the general public. Dr. Kohli's brand transcends professional contexts precisely because she wrote about her lived experiences.

Dr. Kohli's journey demonstrates how writing a book can foster both personal and professional growth. The process—from research to publicity—strengthens communication skills, expands knowledge, and develops new abilities. These pursuits, which may be difficult to pursue while focused solely on clinical practice, can open doors to leadership roles, speaking engagements, and academic collaborations.

The journey of authorship is not only about sharing practices or case studies—it is about realizing the transformative educational value of your knowledge.

Your book can bridge therapeutic literature with broader movements of social change: stories of emotional resilience, creative practice, and compassionate leadership that deeply touch readers.

Therapist-authors must also delve thoroughly into the subjects they choose, conducting in-depth research, exercising critical thinking, and engaging in self-reflection throughout the writing process. This deeper investigation fosters a more comprehensive understanding of their field and often leads to greater clarity and confidence in their therapeutic identity and mission.

New Skills and Opportunities

Writing a book requires a wide range of skills, including researching, writing, editing, effective communication, and outreach and promotion. As a therapist, you have the opportunity to develop and master these skills as you embark on your writing journey. These acquired skills increase your overall professional potential. They are transferable and open doors to leadership roles, speaking engagements, workshops, and academic collaborations.

Once you finish writing a book, few things match the sense of accomplishment you feel afterward. It reflects your persistence and dedication, and this success naturally strengthens both your personal and professional identity. It affirms your expertise and your long-term commitment to the field.

As readers engage with your material and connect personally with the concepts you share, it validates your professional journey. Validation from peers and clients enhances your confidence and deepens your sense of purpose.

Therapists are often encouraged to sound more confident in their opinions, and the act of publishing amplifies their clinical perspectives by providing external recognition.

Writing a book also tests your perseverance, focus, and conviction. Challenges such as writer's block, self-doubt, or harsh criticism from others can feel discouraging, but overcoming them builds lasting confidence and resilience. Each small victory compounds into a greater sense of self-worth—adding immense satisfaction to your career.

Publishing a book can also lead to new professional opportunities. Recognition as an authority and thought leader puts you in a position to attract invitations for speaking engagements, media appearances, consulting roles, teaching positions, and collaborations with other mental health professionals.

A well-written book has an impact that goes far beyond its immediate audience. It can reach therapists, educators, researchers, and even journalists, connecting people across settings, institutions, and borders. Your book becomes a catalyst that expands your professional network and influence, much like a ripple effect.

New opportunities may also arise in mentoring, educating, or supervising new therapists. It can even lead to stipends, paid opportunities, or a transition into part-time or full-time writing, along with roles in public mental health education. Authoring a book is powerful because it creates transformation on two levels: the transformation your readers experience through your words, and the transformation you undergo as new opportunities align with your purpose.

Brand Development

Therapists today are increasingly seeking to establish their professional identity by building strong personal brands. One of the most effective ways to achieve this is by publishing a book.

A book allows you to clearly convey your philosophies, values, and clinical use of effective techniques, while also serving as powerful proof of your expertise and credibility.

Through thoughtful storytelling, ethically shared case studies, and innovative perspectives, your book positions you as a respected expert in the mental health field. Beyond enhancing your influence, it elevates your reputation among peers, clients, and the wider community.

As an author, you gain opportunities for collaborations, media coverage, lectures, and speaking engagements. Your name becomes associated with meaningful ideas and practices, increasing your visibility and expanding your reach. Since your book also provides space to share your journey—the challenges you've faced and the lessons you've learned—your personal brand feels authentic, relatable, and trustworthy.

Most importantly, writing a book enables you to articulate your mission and values in a way that aligns your public persona with your true professional self. Your reputation is then built not only on referrals or credentials but also on a clearly expressed purpose and message.

In short, for any therapist who aspires to lead, inspire, and leave a legacy, a book can serve as the foundation of a strong and enduring personal brand.

> **Your One Message to the World**
>
> Before you write, take some time to reflect. If your book could leave one lasting message, what would it be?
>
> What is the most essential truth you want your clients to remember?
>
> What misunderstanding about your field do you wish to correct?
>
> What idea or insight do you believe could help others heal?
>
> Think about it this way: *"If I had just one message to share with the world through my work as a therapist, it would be..."*

Creating a Sense of Fulfillment

Writing a book offers a window into a therapist's core, providing the chance to reflect on wisdom gained and meaningful experiences throughout their career. In doing so, therapists gain a unique ability to influence the emotional and psychological lives of readers long after they've put the book down. By sharing your knowledge, you contribute to the broader conversation in mental health and create a lasting professional legacy.

Completing a book marks a powerful milestone. It demonstrates commitment, discipline, and even self-advocacy—going far beyond clinical hours or certifications. A book validates your growth as a practitioner and thought leader, boosting your confidence and affirming the value of your unique contributions. Many authors describe the profound sense of accomplishment that comes with seeing their work in print, knowing it will support clients, inspire peers, or educate students. There is also a deeper reward in the act of writing itself—combined with the anticipation of how your words might impact someone's recovery journey.

Ultimately, publishing a book as a therapist is more than a professional achievement. It is a declaration of your commitment to helping others, a tangible expression of your therapeutic identity, and a legacy that endures far beyond the therapy room.

> *"Owning our story and loving ourselves through that process is the bravest thing that we'll ever do."*
>
> — **Brene Brown**

Words from the Authors...

In her memoir *Bibliotherapy in the Bronx,* licensed clinical social worker **Emely Rumble** states that "books were the first therapists" for both herself and her clients. Her writing serves as an excellent example of the therapeutic use of literature. In an Interview with Alexis Jones titled 'Maybe You Need a Bibliotherapist', Emely states:

"*Books were the first place I felt fully mirrored. They were my first therapists, in a way... reading has helped me grieve, hold complexity, process trauma, and reclaim joy.*"

Writing a book is one of the most meaningful contributions a therapist can make—not only to their profession, but to the world at large. If you have a story to tell, a method that works, or a message that deserves to be heard, the written word becomes your bridge. It carries your voice beyond the walls of your practice, reaching people you may never meet, yet whose lives you can profoundly influence.

Your contributions are worthy of recognition, reading, and remembrance. The work of a therapist, clinician, or counselor is grounded in heart, experience, and profound humanity.

The opportunity to extend that healing far beyond the therapy room is tremendous. Whether your goal is to grow your practice, strengthen your brand, shape your profession, or simply share your truth, authorship offers a journey that is both deeply personal and widely impactful. If you have been waiting for the right moment to begin, let this be it. The world needs your voice.

Key Takeaways

- Writing a book brings deep personal and professional rewards to you as a therapist.

- It's a powerful tool for expressing your voice and evolving both personally and professionally.

- Through authorship, therapists can solidify their legacy, enhance their impact, and experience lasting fulfillment.

At Stardom Books, we've had the honor of working with therapists, including clinicians, counselors, psychologists, and social workers — each with a unique message, method, or story to share. What we've seen time and again is this: every therapist has something meaningful to offer, and no two voices are ever the same. Some write to transform, others to teach, and many to simply tell the truth — but all of them create a legacy that outlives the therapy room.

If this chapter has sparked something in you — an idea, a memory, a message you know the world needs — then maybe it's time to take the next step. Our **Clarity Sessions** are designed to help you explore that spark. We'll help you shape your message, map out your vision, and determine whether now is the right time to bring your book to life.

Your voice is powerful. Whether it is sharing your experiences of resilience, introducing a new therapeutic model, or reflecting on your previous work, writing allows you to shape your private wisdom into a public process. It is also a transformative journey. It requires being vulnerable, courageous, and transparent – all of which you have developed as a result of your work as a therapist. The page is a space for healing — now, it's yours.

Your story is valid. Your insight is powerful. And your words have the potential to change more lives than you know.

Chapter 6

STRATEGIC COMMUNITY GROWTH

"What is most personal is most universal."

—**Carl Rogers**

Books are therapy before therapy begins. Long before a client steps into your office, they've already googled their symptoms, watched Reels about trauma, and silently compared therapists online. But the moment they pick up *your* book, something shifts. They experience a form of therapy before therapy—a connection that makes them feel seen, understood, and guided.

Your book is more than pages. It is presence. When your voice sits on their nightstand, in their home, or in their mind, you're no longer just a provider—you've already become a trusted guide.

In today's world, a book is one of the most powerful ways for a therapist to create impact, build trust, and establish credibility. It opens doors to speaking, teaching, consulting, and visibility—but more importantly, it opens the door to healing, starting on the page.

This isn't about selling. It's about resonance. Your book carries your message, your influence, and your legacy—long after the final page is turned.

When therapist Dr. Thema Bryant, a clinical psychologist and president of the American Psychological Association, published her book *Homecoming: Overcome Fear and Trauma to Reclaim Your Whole, Authentic Self*, it began a movement that went beyond individual healing. The empathetic way in which Dr. Thema blended psychology, spirituality, and cultural relevance was  deeply relatable to readers struggling with trauma and identity. Dr. Thema gained a devoted following on social media due to her success, especially from her live events and the podcast "Homecoming." Her writings sparked vibrant online debates, healing circles, and group programs where readers became active participants in an expanding therapeutic community. Dr. Thema did more than educate by putting her book at the center of her message; she also created a connection, trust, and a healing space that extended far beyond the therapy sessions.

Lead Generation: Attracting the Right Clients Through Authorship

For therapists who want to maximize and improve their work, a book can be much more than just a book. A book is a tactical tool. It illustrates your expertise and attracts your next clients, colleagues, and referral sources. When your book speaks to the real needs and concerns of its intended audience, it not only generates interest but also elevates you in the consideration set as an authoritative person.

You can amplify your reach and build rapport by:

- **Distributing your book at conferences**, workshops, community events, or as a free online resource.

- **Including a clear call-to-action** to encourage readers to book sessions, join group programs, or subscribe to your mailing list.

- **Sharing excerpts** from your book on social media, blog posts, or email newsletters to offer bite-sized insights that reflect your therapeutic style.

- **Building momentum through consistent content sharing**, which draws in aligned clients and strengthens your brand presence over time.

Writing a book is not just a side project—it's a high-leverage tool for attracting ideal clients and opening doors to new professional opportunities.

Book as a Client Magnet

A thoughtfully constructed and well-positioned book becomes a comprehensive portrait of your practice. It conveys your values, showcases your experience, and reflects your therapeutic style. Long before a client meets you, it demonstrates your expertise and begins building connections with clients, partners, and even potential investors.

Consider the example of a therapist who specializes in adolescent anxiety. She writes a book on the subject and offers a free downloadable chapter on her website. The chapter speaks directly to parents' most pressing concerns when seeking support for their teens. What happens next? Inquiries begin to rise. Parents feel heard, informed, and more confident about moving forward with treatment.

This example illustrates how a well-crafted book connects powerfully with its intended audience. It attracts the clients most aligned with your message while positioning you as a trusted authority. For collaborators and partners, your book also serves as a clear embodiment of your mission and expertise, opening doors to speaking engagements, referrals, and joint initiatives.

Ultimately, your book doesn't just tell your story—it draws in your ideal audience and communicates your values and vision with clarity.

Case study: Dr. Michele Weiner-Davis

Dr. Michele Weiner-Davis is a world-renowned relationship therapist, speaker, and bestselling author, specializing in marriage therapy and divorce prevention. She is the creator of the "Divorce Busting" method of marriage therapy and the author of multiple books, such as *Divorce Busting, The Sex-Starved Marriage,* and *Healing from Infidelity.* Her book struck a chord with thousands of readers by tackling a very real but frequently overlooked problem—intimacy issues in committed relationships—and encouraged them to seek her advice. Her book positioned her as a trusted authority in her field. Colleagues in her profession started to reach out to her to explore co-creating programs, workshops, and other collaborations. As a result, she saw a massive increase in inquiries from potential clients. This book not only highlights Dr. Michele's clinical talent but also establishes an easy way for prospective clients and collaborators to find her work. Her success demonstrates that a well-written book can draw in your ideal clients and collaborations!

Incorporating Your Book into a Marketing Campaign

Utilizing your book as a **marketing platform** expands your reach and amplifies your message. By promoting its core topics across platforms like social media, email, webinars, and blog posts, you create a unified narrative, demonstrate expertise, and build ongoing audience engagement. Your book becomes a *living tool*—fueling blog content, speaking topics, and social media conversations.

Key takeaways and chapters can be repurposed into blog posts, podcast episodes, video series, or engaging social content. For example, you might:

- Share **bite-sized insights** as Reels or Stories.

- Post short excerpts that spark curiosity.

- Highlight **powerful quotes** with compelling visuals.

- Offer free sample chapters or consultations to your newsletter subscribers or niche online groups.

Collaboration also plays a role. Partnering with thought leaders or influencers in your field increases both visibility and credibility.

Your **website** is another essential tool. It gives future clients a first impression of you and your work. Featuring your book prominently on your homepage, along with testimonials, media coverage, or interviews, strengthens your credibility. Hosting webinars, workshops, or live events based on your book further deepens connections with your audience.

When used strategically, your book becomes more than a publication. It becomes a powerful, portable marketing asset that enhances your brand, attracts ideal clients and partners, and builds lasting relationships.

Another excellent example of using a book as part of a bigger marketing plan is Dr. Lindsay Gibson, a clinical psychologist and author of *Adult Children of Emotionally Immature Parents*. Not only did she conduct webinars based on each chapter of the book and share quotations and short lessons on social media, Instagram, and YouTube, but she also made a free worksheet downloadable on her website. As a result, not only did he book become an Amazon bestseller and was translated into thirteen languages, but she also received an impressive readership on her website and an impressive influx of inquiries into her therapy practice. Her email list grew exponentially, and mental health platforms and podcast hosts began to approach her for features. The book was a magnet for both clients and collaborators because of the intrinsic connection that readers felt to her message before ever speaking with or meeting her.

Revenue Streams: Turning Content into Income

Outside of the conventional therapy room, publishing a book can open up a variety of revenue opportunities. It can lead to paid speaking engagements, consulting work, and the development of workshops or online courses centered around your area of expertise, in addition to book sales.

A well-received book has the potential to generate substantial income, especially if it resonates with a specific audience. Therapists often provide corporate mental health training, lead webinars, or speak at conferences—each a chance to monetize their expertise.

Opportunities for consulting also arise as individuals and organizations seek specialized advice on the frameworks and techniques introduced in your book.

MORO REFLEX
KOKEB GIRMA MCDONALD, OTR/L

The effect lasts beyond the initial sales. Your book is a permanent resource because the material can be used to create the elements of private practice packages, course materials, online programs, or treatment tools. In this way, your book serves as the foundation of your company and brand, generating revenue and laying the groundwork for future expansion.

Kokeb McDonald, a pediatric therapist and author, provides a powerful example of how therapists can leverage book publishing to generate considerable revenue or expand the reach of their profession. McDonald wrote a four-book series called *"Integrating Primitive Reflexes Through Play and Exercise,"* featuring a linear, focused, and client-centered writing style that effectively illustrated her clinical reasoning and practical experience. In addition to captivating her intended audience, the book sold enough to generate over $100,000 in royalties.

Book sales were only one aspect of her success. Her publishing success made her a recognized thought leader in the world of occupational therapy. As her visibility began to increase, organizations began to ask her to speak, facilitate workshops, and consult on how they might use the frameworks she developed in her writing. This is an example of how a good quality book becomes a business tool. By writing a good-quality book, people can create new business revenue and expand their reach in the field.

> **Examples of Community Growth Through Books**
> - **Mailing Lists:** As a result of her book, Dr. Lindsay Gibson received thousands of new subscribers to her newsletter, which contains announcements and resources for follow-up. She also saw a spike in therapy inquiries.
>
> - **Podcast Audiences:** Dr. Thema Bryant transformed the popularity of her book Homecoming into a popular podcast, building audience loyalty and fostering a devoted following that frequently attends her live events and Q&A sessions.
>
> - **Group Programs**: Therapist Kokeb McDonald launched professional training cohorts based on her book. Readers became advocates for her techniques and returned for future workshops.

Enhancing your Brand Visibility

Publishing a book can **dramatically increase the professional visibility and credibility** of a therapist. A book offers value that extends far beyond the therapy room for clients. By publishing, you position yourself as a thought leader—someone who has produced work that is both culturally relevant and intellectually rigorous, while deeply reflective of your therapeutic approach.

Books have staying power. They are cited by scholars, referenced in the media, and discussed at conferences. In this way, your book becomes a professional calling card—a tangible symbol of your expertise that opens doors to new opportunities.

A published book also strengthens your digital presence. Your visibility grows through SEO, social media, and citations as your ideas circulate across platforms. With consistent messaging and alignment between your writing and your professional values, your book enhances your credibility, helping establish you as a known, trusted, and compassionate expert in your field.

Take, for example, Dr. Judith Herman, a psychiatrist and Professor of Psychiatry at Harvard Medical School. Her best-selling book, *Trauma and Recovery*, transformed the field's understanding of trauma and introduced the topic into the mainstream conversation. The book became the foundational text in clinical training and public consciousness, being quoted  and referenced endlessly, especially within the community of academics and researchers, as well as in the media and by policy-makers in the name of human rights. Even now, decades later, the influence of her work continues to yield lecture invitations, interviews, and recognitions. Herman's work helped her gain visibility beyond the four walls of her therapy room to a worldwide conversation on trauma, memory, and justice. She contributed a significant voice in the global effort to humanize and destigmatize trauma survivors through her writing.

Brand Community: Building a Tribe Around Your Message

Before you can fully leverage your book, let us understand what community means in the therapeutic context. For a therapist-author, community can take several forms:

- **Client-facing community**: A Facebook group, mailing list, or therapy group centered around your book and practice.

- **Professional community**: A network of colleagues who use your book as a shared resource for training, case consultation, or oversight.

- **Public audience**: A wider circle that includes people who attend your classes, listen to your podcast, follow you online, and spread the word about your work.

Defining your **ideal community** is essential—it helps you shape the right connections, conversations, and content around your book.

Turning Readers into Advocates

A book is more than a collection of your insights; it's a catalyst for deep discussions that can transform readers into clients, supporters, and advocates. For therapists, this is particularly powerful. When your book touches on emotional or relational struggles, such as trauma, parenting, relationships, or self-worth, it gives readers the sense of being understood. They want to continue the journey beyond the final page.

When you create opportunities for interaction, through book clubs, Facebook groups, or email communities, you provide readers with a way to connect not only with your message but also with one another. This strengthens group identity and positions you as a trusted leader within a values-based community.

You can deepen this engagement further with:
- **Journaling prompts** and reflection exercises.

- **Therapeutic challenges** tied to your book's themes.

- **Discussion topics** for group exploration.

- **Live Q&As, webinars,** or group seminars that extend the learning journey.

These community activities don't just enhance your readers' growth—they expand your reach. Committed readers often become your most passionate advocates, referring you to friends, sharing your work online, and amplifying your visibility. Over time, your audience becomes a natural referral network, reinforcing your mission, credibility, and long-term sustainability as both a therapist and an author.

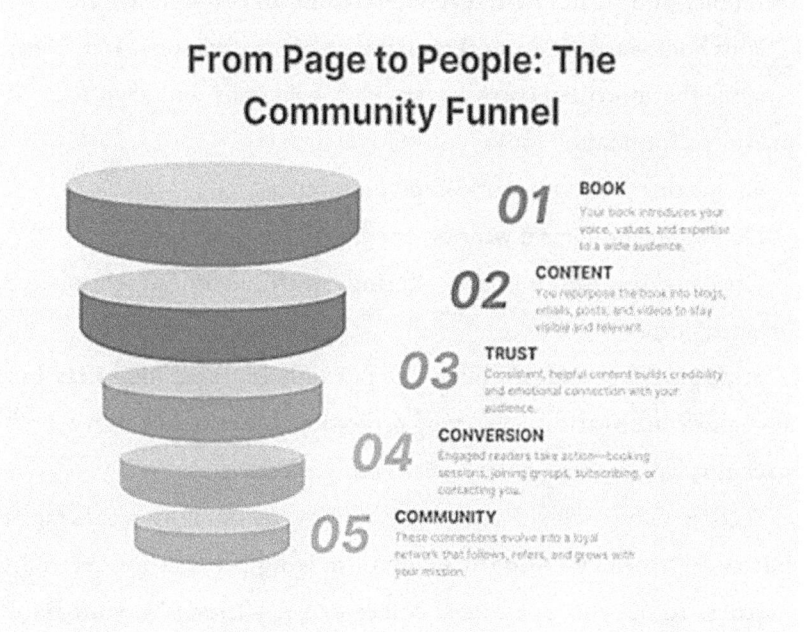

Strategic Partnerships: Collaborate for Greater Impact

Books inherently open doors to **strategic partnerships**—whether with mental health organizations, wellness brands, clinics, schools, or other therapists. When your book conveys your therapeutic philosophy, expertise, and values clearly, it attracts like-minded individuals who want to collaborate to make a meaningful impact.

For example, a therapist who publishes a book on **body image and self-worth** could partner with a yoga instructor and a dietitian to design **holistic wellness retreats**. Together, they could offer workshops and group programs that blend therapy, nutrition, and movement—providing participants with an immersive, transformative experience. This kind of collaboration expands reach, enhances credibility, and creates **new revenue streams** for everyone involved.

Your book acts as a **physical realization of your vision**—something tangible that potential partners can trust, believe in, and align with. It provides a foundation for joint initiatives such as:

Co-hosting webinars, workshops, or seminars.

Developing long-term wellness or educational programs.

Creating interdisciplinary offerings within clinics, schools, or organizations.

Strategic collaborations like these not only **increase visibility** but also **spark innovation**—allowing professionals to amplify each other's strengths while serving communities more effectively.

A compelling, well-written book positions you not only as a therapist but as a **visionary thought leader**—making it easier for the right partners to see you as an ideal collaborator. Ultimately, your book becomes a **bridge**: connecting you with the people, platforms, and initiatives that take your message further than you could ever go alone.

Case Study: Phil Stutz and Barry Michels

The collaboration between Phil Stutz and Barry Michels, writers of *The Tools*, is a striking real-life example of a strategic relationship. Both are psychotherapists; Michels has a background in psychoanalysis, while Stutz has a background in psychiatry. While practicing independently, their mutual desire to make therapy more action-oriented inspired them to collaborate on developing a set of psychological tools to help clients overcome typical mental hurdles. Their book The Tools, published in 2012, consolidated these approaches into a compelling framework so that the general public can understand.

The book not only started a movement but also became a bestseller. Their cooperation went well beyond co-authoring a book:

- **Workshops & Events**: Following the popularity of their book, they began conducting workshops together. It attracted clients seeking practical methods for emotional development, as well as other therapists and coaches.

- **Media & Celebrity Partnerships**: They gained recognition from well-known figures, such as Jonah Hill, which further increased their visibility. As a result of their collaboration, Hill produced the 2022 Netflix documentary *Stutz*, which focused on Phil Stutz and the healing power of the tools. This documentary significantly increased their reach.

- **Therapeutic Programs**: They collaborated to create programs and kept expanding their joint brand. Through their collaboration, The Tools emerged as a technique and a well-known brand name in the self-development and wellness industry.

The example of Phil and Stutz illustrates how a single book, along with a collective orientation and values, can create not only awareness and credibility but also set the stage for innovative collaborations, efforts, and global recognition within the mental health field.

Going Beyond the Pages: Maximizing the Potential of Your Book

In addition to the subject matter of your book, there are ways to amplify its impact even further. One powerful strategy is to provide additional content that supports readers in engaging with your ideas beyond the written word.

You might be wondering: *What more can I provide?* The answer lies in creating complementary resources such as masterclasses, training videos, or workbooks that bring your book's lessons to life. By adding bonus interviews, real-world case studies, and printable exercises tailored to your clients, you transform passive readers into active learners, giving them an enriching and practical educational experience.

This approach supports all kinds of learners—auditory, visual, and experiential—while continually reinforcing your main ideas. More importantly, it positions you as a growth-oriented practitioner who genuinely cares about helping others achieve their mental well-being.

The result is deeper trust, stronger commitment, and long-term loyalty from your readers.

Your book is not simply a milestone; it is a message—a bridge connecting you to the people who most need your voice. For therapists, this goes beyond professional achievement. A book becomes a transformational tool, offering validation, connection, and empowerment long before a client ever walks into your office.

When you are intentional with your writing and strategic in positioning your book, you do more than share ideas—you expand your reach, extend your impact, and invite aligned clients, peers, and partners into your ecosystem. In many ways, your book becomes the **front door to your practice**: a handshake before the first meeting, and a ripple of influence that spreads far beyond your own community.

Key Takeaways

- A well-positioned book attracts the right clients, partners, and new professional opportunities.

- A book will expand your reach through targeted marketing and cultivate a community around your message.

- Supplemental content, such as workbooks, videos, and downloads, enhances impact and caters to diverse learning styles.

- Books can lead to new revenue streams, such as paid speaking engagements, online courses, consulting, and productized services.

- Your book signals your vision and expertise, making collaboration easier and more meaningful.

This isn't about becoming a bestselling author for the sake of ego. It's about reaching the people who need what only *you* can offer—on a scale that clinical hours alone can't sustain. It's about creating assets that work for you while you're resting, building trust while you're working, and leaving a lasting impression that continues to grow even when you're offline.

You're not just writing a book. You're building a business. A brand. A body of work that stands for something and stands the test of time.

Chapter 7

How & Where to Get Professional Help

"When we speak, we are afraid our words will not be heard or welcomed. But when we are silent, we are still afraid. So it is better to speak."

— **Audre Lorde**

As a therapist, you've built your career on listening with intention, creating space for growth, and guiding people through some of the most challenging moments in their lives. You've established a practice, developed systems that work, and helped countless clients move toward healing.

But your expertise doesn't have to stay confined within the four walls of your practice. The insights, frameworks, and lessons you've developed over years of work can benefit a much broader audience. Writing a book allows you to share that knowledge in a way that informs, educates, and supports people you may never meet.

Authorship does more than produce a published work—it expands your impact. A book can enhance your professional credibility, open doors to speaking or teaching opportunities, and establish you as a thought leader in your field. Most importantly, it ensures that your ideas continue to reach readers long after your final session or workshop.

This chapter will help you take what you already do so well in the therapy room and translate it into the written word.

With the right support, you can craft a book that reflects your expertise, extends your influence, and reaches an audience far beyond your immediate practice.

You already know how powerful your words can be in session. Now, imagine what they could do on the page—where they can travel further, last longer, and impact more lives than you could ever see firsthand.

Why a Strategic Publishing Partner Is Essential

It takes more than just putting words on a page to publish a book. It's about creating something significant—transforming your message, experience, and story into something that will last forever. That's why choosing the right publishing partner is so important.

As a therapist, you understand the power of the right container. A safe space can make a world of difference for a client. The same applies to your book. Your ideas need the proper support, the right structure, and the right team to bring them to life. Writing alone is hard. Publishing alone can feel overwhelming. But you don't have to do it alone.

A strategic publishing partner does more than help you finish your manuscript. They help you shape your message, stay focused, and ensure your voice remains clear and strong. They walk with you from start to finish—from your very first idea to the moment your book reaches readers.

At Stardom Books, we recognize the importance of your work. We've helped therapists, coaches, and healers turn their knowledge into books that educate, inspire, and make a real impact. Our process guides you without ever taking over your voice or your vision. We provide the support you need to stay grounded and confident, even when things feel unclear.

Publishing your book is part of your greater purpose. It's not just about having your name on a cover. It's about stepping into your role as a leader—and serving more people than you could ever reach in the therapy room. You already have the wisdom. We help you put it into words that work.

What a Publishing Coach Does

Coming up with the idea of writing a book may sound exciting, but it can quickly feel overwhelming. Therapists are experts at taking on other people's challenges, but when it comes to writing a book, the project often feels daunting. Where do you start? What should you say? How do you write in a way that makes sense to readers who aren't sitting in your office? This is where a publishing coach can add real value.

A good coach provides structure by helping you shape your ideas into a clear book format. They'll ensure your book has a beginning, middle, and end, and help you create a roadmap for moving forward so you don't feel aimless or stuck. A coach brings clarity, helping you uncover and refine your core message.

They ask the right questions, challenge your assumptions, and guide you toward what you truly want to say. Even if you already know your message, a coach will help you sharpen it so it becomes clearer, stronger, and more focused.

Just like in therapy, accountability remains crucial. A coach helps you stay focused, ensuring you don't wonder if you are progressing correctly, because someone is there to offer feedback, support, and encouragement, especially during stressful times or moments of doubt.

While therapists are trained to hold space for others and possess deep knowledge and insight, writing a book differs from practicing therapy.

A coach helps transform professional wisdom into accessible language, making it understandable to everyone, not just specialists.

Here's a simple framework to show how a coach supports you:

- **Clarity** – What is your message? What are you trying to say? Who are you writing for? What do they need to hear?

- **Craft** – How do you say it in a way that connects? How do you share stories, insights, or lessons so they're easy to follow and make a real impact?

- **Confidence** – How do you keep going when self-doubt shows up? How do you finish the book even when you feel unsure, busy, or stuck?

A coach brings all of this together. They help you write a book that feels true to you. A book that sounds like your voice. A book that benefits others even when you are not there. Not even the most famous books had a flawless beginning. Consider *To Kill a Mockingbird*. It wasn't the book we know today when Harper Lee first turned in the manuscript. It was disorganized. Incomplete. Not so much a novel as a series of stories.

However, her editor, Tay Hohoff, recognized something unique in both her and it. For two years, they collaborated to create the book. Hohoff helped Lee find the story's true heart, refine its message, and bring its themes into focus. Without that steady support, To Kill a Mockingbird might never have become the classic it is now.

That's what the right coach or editor can do: they don't take over your voice, but help you strengthen it — and they don't change your message, but help you say it clearly and with impact. Sometimes we just need someone who sees the potential and walks with us to the finish line.

With the right coach, you don't just write. You grow. You become clear, focused, and ready to lead through your words.

How to Choose the Right Coach for You

The ideal coach selection requires evaluating these seven essential factors:

- **Shared Values:** A good coach should feel like someone you can be real with. If you work in a calm, intuitive way, but your coach pushes hard deadlines and pressure, it may not work well. If you value connection and reflection, but they only care about fast results, you may feel dismissed. Look for someone who sees your process and respects it.

- **Real Results:** Ask yourself: has this coach done what I want to do? Have they helped others do it? The best coaches have walked the path and have real experience. They've written books. They've coached others through it. They understand the bumps in the road, not just the theory.

- **Lived Experience and Professional Skills:** A coach with both education and hands-on experience can help you navigate the writing process in a grounded way. You want someone who knows the publishing world and also knows how to work with people, especially people who do deep, emotional work like you.

- **Client Reviews:** Look at who they've worked with. Read their reviews. Are their past clients people like you? Therapists? Coaches? Helpers? Do they speak about feeling supported, seen, and empowered? That says a lot.

- **Aligned Process:** Some coaches use rigid systems. Others are more flexible. Ask what their process looks like. Does it match how *you* work best? Writing should feel meaningful, not mechanical. The right coach creates a process that fits your rhythm, not the other way around.

- **Resilience and Empathy:** A coach who's faced real challenges brings a deeper level of empathy. If they've struggled, failed, and still persevered, they can offer grounded advice when your fears or doubts arise. Their journey matters just as much as yours.

- **Growth Check-ins:** Writing takes time. After a few weeks or a couple of months, the point may arrive when you stop and ask: Is this working? Am I growing? Does this coach still feel like a good fit? It's okay to halt your work from time to time, step back, reassess, and even change direction altogether. That does not qualify as quitting. Instead, it is about ensuring your progress. Choosing a coach is an important decision; trust your gut. Look for someone who makes you feel safe, supported, and strengthened. You are doing important work, and your coach must respect this with you every step of the way. Let's analyze some examples of coaches.

- **Right Fit Example:** You are writing about burnout in therapy. Your coach has worked with mental health professionals before. They let you write in your voice but help you stay clear and on track. You feel safe, heard, and challenged in a good way.

- **Misfit Example:** You are writing about trauma-informed care. Your coach pushes you to "make it more exciting" and ignores your boundaries around language. You leave calls feeling more confused than clear.

Understanding Your Publishing Options: Traditional, Self, and Hybrid

Different therapeutic methods exist, together with various book publication methods. Some are more structured. Some are more flexible. And some offer a balanced, integrative approach.

The process of publishing resembles the three therapy modalities:

- **Traditional publishing** is akin to psychoanalysis: formal, structured, and slow, yet respected.

- **Self-publishing** is like person-centered therapy led by the client (or author), fully flexible, but with little outside guidance.

- **Hybrid publishing** is like integrative therapy —a mix of structure and freedom, where you receive support while still leading the process.

Selecting the one that feels best for you, your book, and your objectives can be made easier if you are aware of these three options.

- **Traditional Publishing**: This is the old-world approach. The process starts by submitting your book proposal to major publishers. They accept responsibility for editing, design, printing, and marketing after they accept your work. The entry into publishing typically requires having an agent to represent you.

Pros:
- Strong name recognition
- No upfront cost
- Built-in distribution

Cons:
- Very competitive
- Loss of creative control
- Long timelines (1–2 years)
- Small royalties

Best for: Authors with a large platform, media connections, or a very commercial idea.
- **Self-Publishing:** You do everything yourself or hire professionals to assist you. You own the whole process and keep complete control. This is the fastest and most flexible option, but also the most work.

Pros:
- Full creative control
- Fast publishing timeline
- Higher royalties

Cons:
- Can be overwhelming
- Quality varies depending on who you hire
- You do all the marketing

Best for: Therapists who prefer a very hands-on approach, want complete control, and are comfortable managing numerous details.

- **Hybrid Publishing:** This model provides you with both worlds simultaneously. You receive expert assistance through editing and design services, yet maintain complete control over your voice and creativity. The publishing house guides the entire process after you make your initial investment.

Pros:
- Shared workload
- High-quality product
- Creative freedom and expert guidance
- Faster than traditional

Cons:

- Requires financial investment

- Not all hybrid publishers are equal — research is important

Best for: Therapists who want support, clarity, and quality, without giving up their voice or waiting years to publish.

Each path has its strengths. However, for many therapists, hybrid publishing is the most sensible option. It allows you to stay true to your message while ensuring your book is polished and professional.

You don't have to figure everything out on your own, and you don't have to give up control either.

Why Hybrid Publishing Works for Therapists

Hybrid publishing is like integrative therapy. It combines the best aspects of various methods. You get the structure of traditional publishing, the freedom of self-publishing, and the professional support that makes the whole process smoother and more effective.

As a therapist, this approach may feel the most natural to you. Why? Because it mirrors how you work. You meet your clients where they are. You don't just follow a script — you bring together different tools to serve the person in front of you. That's precisely what hybrid publishing does.

- **You Keep Your Voice:** Your voice is your power. In therapy, you help clients find their truth and express it in their own words. In publishing, it should be the same. Hybrid publishing respects your voice. You don't have to write in a way that doesn't sound like you. You don't lose control of your message. You get to say what matters most — your way. This is about honoring your voice, just like you honor your clients' autonomy. We don't take over your story. We help you tell it clearly and with impact.

- **You Get Professional Support:** Even the best therapists have supervisors or mentors. Not because they don't know what they're doing, but because reflection and feedback help deepen the work. Hybrid publishing offers that kind of professional guidance for your book. You are not left to figure out editing, layout, or structure on your own. Experienced editors, designers, and book coaches walk with you, step by step. You still lead, but you are not alone.

- **You Don't Have to Do the Marketing Alone:** This is a big one. Most therapists don't enjoy marketing. And that's okay. You already give so much of yourself to your clients and your work. When it's time to share your book with the world, hybrid publishing helps you do so without burning out. At Stardom Books, we help you create an innovative, ethical marketing plan that aligns with your personality and values. You don't have to be loud. You don't have to dance on social media. You just have to show up — and we'll show you how. With this kind of support, you get more time for your clients—or more time to rest. Either way, it's a win.

- **The Process Feels Safe and Grounded:** Writing a book brings up stuff. Imposter syndrome. Fear of judgment. Pressure to sound "perfect." Hybrid publishing provides structure and steady guidance, making the process feel less overwhelming and more manageable. It's not just about the final book. It's about how you feel while making it. You want the journey to match your values, thoughtful, respectful, and aligned.

- **You Build Something That Lasts:** Your Book Isn't Just a Project. It's a legacy. It's a way to reach people outside the therapy room. Whether you want to educate, inspire, advocate, or lead, hybrid publishing helps you build something that will stand the test of time.

And you do it without compromising on quality, integrity, or your voice.

For therapists, hybrid publishing just makes sense. It gives you the structure you need, the freedom you want, and the support you didn't know you were missing.

It's publishing, done the way you work — with intention, care, and real results.

How Stardom Books Serves Therapists Uniquely

Stardom Books is more than just a book publishing company. We form alliances, particularly with therapists. We understand the kind of work you do — and the deep consideration, care, and emotional effort that go into it. For this reason, we approach projects with the same presence, organization, and profound regard for the process that you do with treatment.

We Offer Containment

The practice of therapeutic containment establishes a secure environment. People expand their development when they experience protective support. Writing follows the same principle. Writing a book without proper direction results in scattered chaos and overwhelming difficulty. The process starts to flow when someone supports you throughout the writing journey.

Our publishing team gives you that container. From outlining your book to editing your final draft, we walk beside you. We don't rush you. We don't force your message into someone else's formula. We help you build something true to your work and your voice.

We Reflect and Refine (Like Mirroring)

In the therapy room, mirroring helps clients gain insight into themselves. It brings insight and clarity. That's what our editors and coaches do with your writing. We read with care. We reflect what we see. We ask questions. We help shape your message without changing your tone.

This is not about fixing you. It's about helping your book shine while staying authentic.

You've already thought. We help you express it in a way that connects with people outside the therapy room — in a voice that sounds like you.

We Help You Position Your Voice

Therapists often avoid labeling themselves as experts even though they have this status. You possess insights and wisdom that others need, even though you feel you are not a thought leader. Your book exists beyond its collection of ideas. Your book serves as a tool that establishes your position as a dependable leader in your specialized field.

Our team helps you develop a message structure that enhances the visibility of your voice. This is not about ego, it's about clarity.

Through our guidance, more people will discover you and believe in your message to the world.

We will assist you in utilizing your book to create opportunities that lead to ideal client attraction, as well as speaking invitations and influence within your professional domain.

We Take Care of the Details

You don't need to learn cover design, page layout, or Amazon strategy. We handle the technical side so you can stay focused on the parts that matter most to you — your message, your story, your clients.

From formatting to distribution, we've got you covered. We ensure your book looks good, reads well, and reaches the right audience in both print and digital formats.

We also help with marketing in a way that feels natural. You won't be asked to "sell yourself" in ways that feel fake or loud. Instead, we guide you in building authentic visibility based on your values, tone, and strengths.

We've Helped Others Like You

We have many authors who are therapists, coaches, and healers. They brought ideas that felt too big, too messy, or too vulnerable to share. Together, we helped refine those ideas into published books that share meaningful insights with readers worldwide.

Some are building private practices, and some are launching courses, keynotes, and movements. Each of them was just like you; they started with a story.

At Stardom Books, we're not just a publisher. We're a partner. We listen. We guide. We hold the space so you can do the work only you can do. And when your book is ready, we help it meet the world.

From Page to Platform: The Authority Influencer Roadmap

Writing a book is not just about the book. It's about what comes after. For many therapists, a book becomes more than words on a page — it becomes a platform. It builds your credibility. It expands your reach. It helps you stand out in a crowded field. And most importantly, it helps more people find and trust your work.

At Stardom Books, we guide you through what we call the **Authority Influencer Roadmap**. This is a simple, three-part process: **Plan, Build, Launch.** Each stage helps you move from an idea in your head to a published book that opens new doors in your career.

- **Plan: Know Who You Are Talking To:** Before you start writing, you need clarity. Who is this book for? What do they need from you? What kind of transformation are you offering? As a therapist, this is where you define your niche. It could be individuals experiencing burnout, couples in crisis, or trauma survivors. This is your chance to speak directly to them, outside the therapy room.

We help you clarify your message and your audience. That way, your book feels focused and intentional, not vague or scattered.

- **Build: Shape Your Voice and Message:** Now that you know who you are writing for, it's time to build your message. This is where your authority starts to grow.

We help you take your insights and turn them into content that feels useful and strong. You don't just write your book — you also begin shaping how the world sees you.

For example:

o If you are known for trauma work, your book becomes a trusted resource in that space.

o If you help couples reconnect, your book becomes part of your brand.

o If you want to train others, your book can open the door to speaking and teaching.

You're not merely creating pages, but establishing your presence.

- **Launch: Share It with the World:** This is the moment everything comes together. Your book is done. It's ready to meet your readers.

But launching a book isn't just about hitting "publish." It's about using the book to grow your impact. We help you think through how to share your message in a way that feels natural and aligned.

For many therapists, their book becomes:

- A referral tool for their practice

- A way to start workshops or speaking gigs

- A way to reach clients before they even enter the room

You already have something important to say. The Authority Influencer Roadmap helps you say it — clearly, powerfully, and with purpose. Let your book become the bridge between your private work and your public voice.

Your Next Step

You already hold knowledge that helps people heal. Now is the time to let your voice travel further, through a book that reflects who you are and what you stand for.

If you feel called to write but aren't sure where to begin or how to move forward, we invite you to speak with a Stardom Books Publishing Advisor.

It's an intensive conversation.

Think of it like a first session with a new client — a space to explore, ask questions, and see if we're the right fit. We'll talk about your goals, your ideas, and what kind of support would help you most. This is a pressure-free space focused on clarity.

Many therapists tell us this first call was the moment everything started to feel real. It gave them focus. It gave them momentum. And sometimes, it permitted them to take the next step.

If you are ready to talk, we're ready to listen.

Schedule your Clarity Session here:

stardombooks.com/clarity-session

Harper Lee experienced a similar journey with her writing. The manuscript she submitted originally lacked the familiar structure that would eventually become *To Kill a Mockingbird*. The book required both time and dedicated support, as well as an editor who understood her unique voice, before it became *To Kill a Mockingbird*.

The same is true for you.

Over the years, you've guided people through transformation and tough decisions, offering support when others couldn't. Such an experience holds tremendous value.

Such valuable work needs to exist outside the boundaries of your professional practice.

Your book is a way to keep helping even when you are not in the room. It can reach people you'll never meet. It can speak on your behalf when you are resting, teaching, or working with someone else. That's the beauty of writing. It multiplies your impact.

You don't need to do this alone. You already know how to hold others. Let someone hold this process for you.

You've helped so many people. Now let your book help more.

Putting It All Together

"Writing a book is a tremendous experience. It pays off intellectually. It clarifies your thinking. It builds credibility. It is a living engine of marketing and idea spreading, working every day to deliver your message with authority. You should write one."

—— **Seth Godin**

If you've made it to this point in the book, it means something important: you're no longer just thinking about writing a book—you're seriously considering it. Maybe for the first time, for the tenth—but you're still here. That means the idea has taken hold.

The process of authorship is a transformative journey and a strategic professional tool. Writing a book strengthens your voice, widens your reach, and clarifies your work and communication. Therapists who take this step share a wish to create meaningful work that transforms lives.

Now you stand at the start of your journey.

The journey that lies ahead has ceased to be theoretical. It's real. The next step has shifted from theoretical understanding to practical implementation. It's about taking concrete steps toward your goals.

To summarize, the main takeaways are: Writing a book helps clarify your voice, enhances your professional impact, and demonstrates your ideas in action. Reflect on these insights as you plan your next steps.

The Value of the Book

Writing a book is more than a personal achievement; it's a strategic investment in your professional future and a way to build your standing. Authorship enhances your professional status, deepens client connections, and expands your network. Many therapists have found these benefits to be genuine in their own experiences.

Writing a good book establishes you as an expert. Clients, colleagues, and your community recognize that your insights have a broader impact. Your ideas, born from client sessions, reach broader audiences: students, media, organizations, and future clients.

It also deepens the way you communicate. Many therapists find that writing helps them clarify their frameworks, answer frequently asked questions, and give clients something tangible to return to—something that lives on after the session ends. A book can serve as both a teaching tool and a means of building trust.

And beyond all that, there is personal transformation. Writing a book forces you to distill what you believe, what you've learned, and how you want to be seen in the world. It's a mirror as much as a message. You may begin your manuscript thinking it's about helping others (and it is), but you'll find it also reveals and reaffirms the deepest parts of your why. This personal growth is an exciting part of the journey.

Your primary purpose in writing is not just to provide information. Instead, your writing helps build connections, support others, and create work that will last.

The book you are writing or working on exists beyond its physical form because it represents your legacy. Through this work, you express your voice while it travels across space. Through this vehicle, your message extends past what you could accomplish on your own.

Taking the First Step

Every book begins with a moment of decision. The creation of a book begins when someone decides to start writing, rather than starting with an outline or a title.

You don't need to have everything figured out. You don't need to know your table of contents by heart, or whether this book will be part memoir, part manual, or something in between. What you need is intention. Who are you writing for? What do you want them to understand, feel, or do as a result of reading your words? What matters most in what you have to say? This intention will guide you and keep you focused on your goal.

The rest unfolds from there.

It's natural to feel hesitation. Doubts will show up. You may wonder whether your voice is unique enough, whether your story is significant, or whether now is the right time. That's not a sign to stop—it's a sign you're taking this seriously. Every author starts there. What is the difference between those who write and those who only think about writing? Willingness. Not fearlessness. Just willingness.

Start small. Choose one story you want to tell. One client moment that shifted your perspective. One insight you return to again and again in your sessions. Use that as your spark. Don't try to write the whole book in a weekend. Set a writing rhythm that fits your real life—whether that's fifteen minutes a day or two hours every Saturday morning.

Allow yourself to create work that is not perfect. The first draft is not about perfection; it is about making progress and being honest. You can always shape, improve, and eventually publish it.

Through their education, therapists learn how to help people develop and undergo personal transformations.

Your path to writing a book mirrors the same transformation process that therapists use with their clients. There will be resistance. There will be doubt. But there will also be clarity, purpose, and breakthroughs.

Through your actions, you have positively transformed numerous people. Writing a book helps your impact reach further. The first step is not about mastery. It's about movement.

You don't have to be fearless.

You just have to begin.

Collaboration is Power

Writing can feel like a solitary process, but it doesn't have to be. It shouldn't be.

Much like therapy, authorship is most potent when it's collaborative. While the message must be yours, the process doesn't need to rest solely on your shoulders. You guide your clients through transformation every day—you don't expect them to walk their path alone. The same applies to you as an author. A powerful book is rarely the result of a lone effort. It's built through meaningful partnerships.

From idea to publication, some professionals can support every step of your writing journey. Book coaches help shape your ideas and keep you accountable. Editors sharpen your message, strengthen your voice, and ensure your words resonate with the reader. Designers, formatters, and marketing strategists transform your manuscript into a polished product that reflects your brand. And hybrid publishers offer the structure, experience, and professional insight of a traditional team, while preserving your ownership and vision.

The truth is, working with the right people doesn't dilute your voice—it protects it. It helps you write faster and better, and it allows you to stay grounded in your zone of genius while others guide the parts of the process you weren't trained for. Collaboration turns the dream of a book into a realistic, achievable timeline.

Licensed therapist Liz Fiedorow Sjaastad began her writing journey through private journaling, which served as a therapeutic practice. The writing project began as an intimate personal investigation into her family trauma, which included her mother's schizophrenia and her father's WWII silence, as well as her processing of these events. The initial writing purpose did not include publication as part of its plan. Through her writing development, Liz discovered that her narrative could potentially offer assistance to others.

When traditional publishing felt inaccessible and restrictive, Liz chose the hybrid route. Through Wise Ink Media, she partnered with experts who helped her refine her voice, design her cover, shape her message, and position her memoir for the people who needed it most. The result was *You're Too Young to Understand*—a book that stayed true to her story and reached readers in meaningful ways.

Liz didn't have to compromise her voice to get her message out. She had help, but she stayed in control. That's the power of collaboration.

You don't have to figure it out alone. You don't have to wear every hat. As in therapy, the work remains yours, but this process becomes so much better when shared.

Publishing Models Simplified

For new authors, publishing often feels confusing, with jargon and choices at every turn. It doesn't have to be. Like therapy approaches, each publishing path—traditional, self, or hybrid—has unique benefits and considerations.

The key is to pick what best matches your voice and goals.

- **Traditional publishing** involves signing with a publisher—often through an agent—who handles production and distribution. You exchange some creative control and revenue for their support, wider reach, and prestige. The process can be slow and competitive, but it suits those seeking structure and broad distribution.

- **Self-publishing** offers complete control over your book's content, design, and marketing, but you manage every aspect, including hiring professionals and covering costs. This route works for those with clear vision and time, but can feel overwhelming for many busy therapists.

- **Hybrid publishing** combines expert support—editing, design, marketing—with your ownership and creative direction. It's an investment, but it delivers professional results without the delays and gatekeeping of traditional publishing.

Hybrid publishing often provides therapists with an ideal balance: your voice is respected, the process is streamlined, and you retain decision-making power—all with professional support.

There's no one best path—choose what fits your needs, goals, and available time. Clarifying your priorities will guide the way.

The Book as a Brand, a Platform, and a Legacy

When you write a book, you're not just publishing words on a page—you're building something much larger: a brand, a platform, and a legacy. Authorship doesn't live in isolation. It becomes woven into how others perceive you, how you perceive yourself, and how your message extends beyond the therapy room.

A book elevates your professional identity. It becomes part of how clients, colleagues, and organizations understand your approach and your expertise. When someone Googles your name, your book becomes part of what they find—and part of why they trust you. It conveys that you've taken the time to reflect, organize your ideas, and offer something meaningful. That alone builds credibility.

But it goes further.

Your book can open doors to speaking engagements, media appearances, brand collaborations, and educational partnerships. Therapists like Dr. Bessel van der Kolk (*The Body Keeps the Score*) and Nedra Glover Tawwab (*Set Boundaries, Find Peace*) didn't just write books—they built platforms. Their words became frameworks, movements, and conversations. Their reach expanded far beyond one-on-one sessions because they created something that could be handed from reader to reader, therapist to client, teacher to classroom.

You don't have to be a viral sensation or a household name to do the same. You just need a book that carries your voice with clarity and heart.

This isn't about becoming famous. It's about becoming accessible. A book allows people to engage with your work on their terms—in their own time. Whether they're clients who aren't ready for therapy, professionals seeking growth, or communities seeking language to express their pain, your book can meet them where they are.

And while a book can certainly create revenue through sales, workshops, or consulting opportunities, the real return is measured in impact. In the people who quote your words. In the invitations you receive.

In conversations, your message sparks discussions that might never have occurred otherwise.

When you write a book, you create something that outlives a single session or a single season of your career. It becomes a lasting part of your contribution. A book teaches. It heals. It reaches.

It becomes your signature.

And over time, that signature becomes a legacy—one only you can leave. Remember, your work shapes how others perceive you, builds trust, and creates a lasting contribution to your field.

What Holds People Back? (And How to Push Through It)

If you're hesitating to start your book—or to keep going—you're not alone. Even the most experienced, insightful therapists struggle with the same doubts:

What if I don't have enough to say? What if it's not good enough? What if I'm not a writer?

These fears don't mean you're unprepared. They mean you care.

Being an excruciatingly exacting learner and perceptive listener, you are supposed to be mindful at all times with your words, to hold space with unerring precision, and never to harm. Care, considered an attribute in clinical work, can occasionally impede the creative process. But here's the truth: Your book doesn't need to be perfectly crafted to be powerful. It needs to be honest. It needs to be useful. It needs to be yours.

Clarity very rarely appears before the work has started. It gives meaning through the process, such as writing the wrong thing before finding the right one, through the pursuit of ideas that convey a significant message.

Writing is a discovery process that reveals what you think, what you believe, and what you are obligated to say.

If you wait until everything feels certain, you may wait forever.

Instead, reframe the goal. Don't write a perfect book. Write a true one. Write the book your clients keep asking for. The one you wish you had when you started. The one that gives language to what others can't yet name.

Let the first draft be messy. Let it be too long or too short. Let it be incomplete because every strong book starts that way—imperfect, but in motion.

You've already walked with clients through discomfort, vulnerability, and growth. Writing a book is your chance to do that for yourself—and eventually, for your readers.

You don't need to feel ready. You just need to be brave enough to begin.

There will never be a perfect moment to write your book.

Life will always be whole. Your schedule will always be full. The idea will never feel quite polished enough. And yet—if you've made it this far, you already know something essential: the opportunity is here. And it's waiting for you to say yes.

You are already qualified to write this book—your experiences, your insights, your clinical wisdom, and your lived humanity all matter. You've walked beside people in their most challenging moments. You've helped them rewrite their own stories. You've gathered lessons and truths that others need to hear.

That is what makes you an author, not literary perfection, not publishing credentials. Voice. Purpose. Perspective.

Writing a book allows your work to expand its reach and create a lasting impact. It is a resource that can travel further and speak to people you may never meet—people who need your guidance. Authorship opens new avenues for reach, meaning, and resonance. You are creating something that lives beyond the moment when a conversation ends.

Building a legacy goes beyond just sharing information. The legacy is shared through the very thinking, philosophy, and rationale of the healer. That is what people tap into. That is what builds trust."

Stop waiting for perfection—act now. Open a new document or jot down your opening lines today. The clarity and momentum you need come from taking the first step. Your book's journey starts with this action. Make it happen now.

Stardom Books helps therapists like you bring books to life. Reach out now to start your path to publication—whether you're brainstorming or revising. Take the next active step today so readers can benefit from your insight. Connect with us and get your story started.

Your Story Is Calling. Let's Begin.

You've done the work. You've clarified your message, deepened your purpose, and envisioned what your book could become. Now, it's time to take that first meaningful step toward bringing it to life.

Schedule your 1:1 Clarity Session with Stardom Books. This personalized, no-pressure conversation will equip you with a tailored plan to turn your book idea—whether it's in early stages or fully drafted—into a clear next step.

- Strategic insight into publishing options that fit your goals, timeline, and voice.

- Expert feedback from a team that specializes in working with therapists and thought leaders.

- Next steps that feel actionable, aligned, and achievable.

You don't have to navigate this process on your own. Your session provides direct, actionable guidance and personalized clarity so you can move forward with confidence, knowing exactly what to do next.

Your story deserves a wider reach. Your message is ready to lead. This is your doorway to the writing journey you've envisioned—and more.

Start here: https://stardombooks.com/clarity-session/

About the Author

RAAM ANAND

5-times Bestselling Author

Publishing Advisor to Top Leadership

Investor in Various Start-ups

Chief Editor & Publisher

High-performance Coach

Raam Anand coaches aspiring authors and non-writers to become published authors, guiding them through the process of completing, launching, and marketing their books. He is a five-time international bestselling author and has been recognized for his leadership coaching.

As the Chief Editor at Stardom Books (USA/India), Raam has published over 260 authors while coaching individuals to enhance productivity, establish personal brands, and successfully publish and promote their books. Official statistics and magazines report that Raam is one of the world's leading publishing coaches.

He has trained thousands of CXOs, experts, entrepreneurs, and thought leaders through his books, online courses, workshops, and conferences.

www.ingramcontent.com/pod-product-compliance
Lightning Source LLC
LaVergne TN
LVHW011422080426
835512LV00005B/214